PUPPETRY AS AN INSTRUCTIONAL PRACTICE FOR CHILDREN WITH

LEARNING DISABILITIES: A CASE STUDY

by

Unoma Bryant Comer

JASON WARD, Ed.D., Faculty Mentor and Chair

JACKSON "SKOT" BEAZLEY, Ed.D., Committee Member

CHERYL DORAN, Ph.D., Committee Member

Barbara Butts Williams, Ph.D., Dean, School of Education

A Dissertation Presented in Partial Fulfillment

Of the Requirements for the Degree

Doctor of Philosophy

Capella University

July 2009

UMI Number: 3360438

INFORMATION TO USERS

The quality of this reproduction is dependent upon the quality of the copy submitted. Broken or indistinct print, colored or poor quality illustrations and photographs, print bleed-through, substandard margins, and improper alignment can adversely affect reproduction.
In the unlikely event that the author did not send a complete manuscript and there are missing pages, these will be noted. Also, if unauthorized copyright material had to be removed, a note will indicate the deletion.

ProQuest LLC
789 East Eisenhower Parkway
P.O. Box 1346
Ann Arbor, MI 48106-1346

Abstract

This qualitative case study research design investigated puppetry as a holistic

constructivist instructional practice for children with learning disabilities that included

puppeteers and special education teachers as coresearchers. The purpose of the study was

to investigate how puppetry can be an effective instructional practice for children with

learning disabilities to promote engagement, participation, and social and emotional well-

being with their nondisabled peers. The study was based on data collected from 9

individual interviews, 5 special education teachers, and 4 professional puppeteers. The

results of the study indicated the teachers and puppeteers believed that students benefit

from the introduction of puppets into the instruction of students with learning disabilities.

The coresearchers also indicated that the introduction of puppetry as an instructional

practice would result in the children's strong self-awareness and acknowledgment of their

disabilities.

Dedication

To all who do sticks, string, wire, board, and cloth to influence a lesson to teach or story to tell.

Acknowledgments

Words cannot express my deepest gratitude. Simply, thank you, Leslie Sue, Dr. Jason, Dr. Skot, Dr. Cheryl, Estelle, Debbie, Paula, Jessie, Dean, 1350, St. James, Jackie H., Jackie T., Jeff, Rita, Jennifer, Elizabeth, Malik, Khaalis, William, Shelia, Pops (1924–2007); for the future, Desmond, Charles Jr., Shaundra, Mikki, Malik Jr., and Jurnee; and Charles.

Table of Contents

List of Tables

CHAPTER 1. INTRODUCTION/STATEMENT OF THE PROBLEM

Introduction to the Study

The field of educating children with learning disabilities is replete with

reductionistic remediation intervention techniques and curriculum designed to assist

children with academic achievement (Mann, 1979; Myers & Hammill, 1976; Myklebust,

1968; Poplin, 1988a). This all began because of the need to help children who were not

allowed to be registered for school because of their learning problems (Lerner, 1971).

Public Law 94-142, the Education of All Handicapped Children Act, was passed in 1975

and structured so that children with disabilities could receive an equal education with

their nonhandicapped peers (Hallahan & Cruickshank, 1973).

Historically, the instructional models underlying special education services have

been deficit-driven, as shown in Poplin (1988a). Poplin described a deficit-driven

curriculum as one in which the child's weaknesses are treated as the basis for instruction.

The field of learning disabilities is replete with the deficit-driven model as a process in

which instruction is based on the understanding that treating a child's weaknesses will

result in academic progress. Poplin explained that the difficulty in using deficit-driven

practices lies with the fact that children with learning disabilities tend to not improve in

their areas of weakness with deficit-driven practices. If the premise of using a child's

strengths were a consideration in instruction, the children with learning disabilities might

show academic improvement or gains, because of the emphasis on their strengths.

Although methods have changed, proposed strategies—even in articles such as Wong's (1988)—tend to be deficit driven. Wong explained remediation from a processing deficit, whereas Hayward, Das, and Janzen (2007) looked at cognitive remediation in their study of programs for reading improvement.

Supporting the need for continuing research, Katz, Stone, Carlisle, Corey, and Zeng (2008) conducted a study of children with learning, speech, and language disabilities. They compared the disabled students' reading scores with nondisabled peers. Their study, conducted over a 2-year period, examined teachers who used literacy curriculum that had been approved by the No Child Left Behind (NCLB) legislation. Results of this longitudinal study indicated that children who required special-education assistance because of their disability did not make the same progress compared to their regular-education, nondisabled peers. Katz et al. stated, "Specifically, children evidenced slower growth within each year on the Oral Reading Fluency Word Analysis, and Listening Comprehension, from the assessments of the Iowa Test of Basic Skills Dynamics Indicators of Basic Early Literacy Skills" (p. 45). The study specifically cited that there was a difference between the two groups.

Puppetry as an Instructional Methodology

This research investigated the use of puppetry as an instructional methodology to teach children with learning disabilities. Currently, the instructional practices in the area of special education specific to children with learning disabilities are structured around a deficit-driven paradigm. The term *deficit-driven* was explained by Poplin (1988a) in her seminal work and Poplin and Cousin (1996) to describe how children with learning disabilities have received instruction in academics. The field is replete with explaining

2

learning disabilities as deficits of skills that children are lacking or do not have (Hallahan

& Cruickshank, 1973; Hammill & Bartel, 1971; Mann, 1979; Myklebust, 1968;

Wiederholt, 1974). Therefore, the tradition has been to remediate special-needs children

with instruction focused on their deficits. All instructional practices were designed

around this remediation process. Remediation is synonymous with deficits in academic

skills. Because the deficit-driven practice (Poplin & Cousin 1996) is still being presented,

even with the new revised statutes of the Individuals with Disabilities Act of 1997

(IDEA), it is apparent that a new paradigm is warranted. Poplin and Cousin pointed out

that a new paradigm is called for because the traditional approach based on their

weaknesses or perceptual deficits does not appear to be beneficial for children with

learning disabilities. Poplin and Cousin's research also presents alternative views that

promote a new paradigm for instruction and curriculum for children with learning

disabilities. Their work is supported by Stone's (1992) dissertation that examined

children with learning disabilities and children who are second-language learners in the

areas of visual artistic creativity.

Stone's (1992) basic premise acknowledged the study of children in a more

holistic manner so that the teacher could acknowledge and focus on the students'

strengths in visual artistic creativity. Stone advocated in her research that children with

learning disabilities and children who spoke English as a second language were equal in

areas of creativity to their nondisabled peers. The results of her dissertation indicated that

not only did the subtest of elaboration as an area of creativity support the hypothesis that

the children with learning disabilities are equal to their nondisabled peers in areas of

divergent thinking and feeling, but also that children with disabilities exceeded their

3

peers in the subtest of humor. Research by Hearne, Poplin, Schoneman, and

O'Shauchnessy (1988) also supports the recognition in the area of technology, promoting

a new paradigm for instruction and curriculum. Based on the previous research regarding

deficit-driven instructional practices, the introduction of puppetry might be seen as a

nondeficit-driven instructional practice to support the work by Poplin and Cousin (1996)

as well as Hearne and Stone (1995).

Gifted With Special Needs

A gifted child with learning disabilities is a subset category under the special

education category of learning disabilities. Children who have learning disabilities but are

also recognized as gifted can receive services in a special education classroom. These

services are usually provided in a resource room environment. Whitmore and Maker

(1985) recognized some famous people in this gifted/learning disabled (G/LD) category,

including Steven Hawkins and Helen Keller. Lovett and Lewandowski (2006) explained

how the population of the gifted and learning disabled student is still not recognized for

their strengths and talents.

Concept of Reductionism

This investigation focused on the movement from remediation intervention

toward a constructivist model for primary instruction. Currently, in practice as well as the

literature, there is still a tendency to instruct children with learning disabilities with a

reductionistic model. This concept of reductionism, originated in the field of learning

disabilities with Myklebust in 1968 and Lerner in 1971, referred to children's processing

abilities to be viewed as weaknesses. These weaknesses, once identified through a battery

of cognitive and affective assessments, were then treated within an instructional

4

framework to be reduced to the smallest unit to be learned. It was believed that children with learning disabilities needed to have instruction broken down to the smallest unit in order to achieve academic success (Mann, 1979; Myers & Hammill, 1976; Myklebust). This study investigated puppetry as a mode of instruction to improve engagement, participation, and social and emotional growth for children with learning disabilities. Historically, puppetry has not been an integral part of the educational landscape, although it has been utilized in a variety of peripheral venues such as television. Because students with learning disabilities require nondeficit, holistic constructivist learning approaches, a study to investigate the utilization of puppetry will provide data to support this premise that nondeficit, holistic constructivist learning approaches are a more effective instructional practice for increasing participation, engagement, and social and emotional growth of children with learning disabilities (Poplin & Cousin, 1996).

Background of the Study

The first federal laws designed to assist and educate individuals with disabilities date back to the earliest days of the United States. In 1798, the Fifth Congress passed the first federal law concerned with the care of persons with disabilities, the Marine Hospital Service, to provide medical services to seamen who were sick or disabled. By 1912, this service became known as the Public Health Service (National Dissemination Center for Children With Disabilities [NICHCY], 2004).

In most of U.S. history, schools have been allowed to exclude and often did exclude certain children, especially those with disabilities (Pub. L. No. 94-142, 1975; U.S. Office of Education, 1977). Since the 1960s, however, there has been a number of federal legislative actions that relate directly or indirectly to individuals with disabilities, particularly children and youth (Lerner, 1971). Looking back over the last 40 years, it is clear that federal protection and guarantees of the educational rights of individuals with disabilities have been an evolving story. As a result of the state and federal laws passed since the 1960s (specifically, P.L. 89-10, Elementary and Secondary Education Act of 1965) and the ensuing court cases that have occurred, children with disabilities now have specific rights protected by law and full access to what is being called a free and appropriate public education, better known as FAPE. These laws have also been the impetus for the creation of an organization called *Kids on the Block*. This organization is designed to provide opportunities for nondisabled children in socializing with their disabled peers through the use of puppetry. Additionally, this organization was formed to assist children with special education needs in their social development as they interact with their peers in the regular education classroom. This was in direct response to P.L. 94-142, the original special education act (U.S. Office of Education, 1968).

Puppetry as an Instructional Tool

Historically, puppetry has been used primarily in the entertainment industry. With the creation of *Sesame Street* in 1969, a new genre of using puppets for instructional purposes became the focus of integrating entertainment and instructional material. Additionally, the organization Kids on the Block and other puppet-based presentations were created to address the needs of children with special education concerns, incorporating entertainment with instructional practices. IDEA requires children with special needs to be placed in the least restrictive environment (LRE). The advent of LRE meant that many disabled children would now receive the majority of their instruction in a regular education setting with their nondisabled peers.

6

The primary purpose of these puppet troupes was to help nondisabled children understand their peers in social situations. Initially, there did not appear to be consideration that Kids on the Block assisted with achievement in areas of engagement and participation. Therefore, this qualitative case study examined how and to what extent puppetry as associated with Kids on the Block and other puppet troupes may formally assist children to improve engagement, participation, and social and emotional growth. The scope of this study included an examination of the benefits of puppetry as a creative instructional strategy.

With the need for additional research to support the tenet that children with learning disabilities can learn in a nondeficit, nonreductionistic manner, according to Poplin and Cousin's (1996) work, it was important to acknowledge the strengths and talents of children academically using a nonremediation approach to instruction. This study investigated aspects of using puppetry as a holistic constructivist mode of instruction to assist children with their participation, engagement, social and emotional growth, and ability to socialize with their peers. The use of puppetry provided a nondeficit, nonremediation approach to instruction. Because children with disabilities are now being taught in a general education classroom, there is a need to help children without disabilities understand and befriend children with special needs.

IDEA, the current acronym for the reestablishment of P.L. 94-142, originally named Education for All Handicapped Children Act, is built around six basic tenets. These tenets include child find (a process to identify children with disabilities), FAPE, nonbiased assessments, a structured IEP (individualized education plan), the right for due process, and the right to have full access to the regular curriculum in the least restrictive environment, also known as LRE (Lewis & Doorlag, 1995).

A new political climate in the United States has established a redevelopment of the original public law for the education for all handicapped children, which was combined with the American with Disabilities Act (ADA) to include children. The new IDEA focuses on the education of individuals from birth until adulthood, which were the original guidelines for P.L. 94-142. IDEA has also added autism to the top 13 federally regulated disabilities.

With the development of P.L. 94-142 and IDEA, the federal government began to address the educational needs for children with disabilities. Public Law 94-142, the Education of All Handicapped Children, passed on November 29, 1975, was established and structured so all children could receive an equal education regardless of their handicapping condition. The law states,

> In order to receive funds under the act, every school system in the nation must make provision for a free and appropriate public education for every child between the ages of 3 and 21 (unless state law does not provide free public education to children 3 to 5 or 18 to 21 years of age) regardless of how seriously they may be handicapped. (P.L. 94-142, p. 3)

Provisions within the law include (a) identification of children, (b) service to them at no cost to parent, (c) rights of the parent to be informed about testing and classifying whereby parents are entitled to disagree and take legal action at the schools' expense, (d) permission of the parent for testing and placement; if none is available, the child is entitled to a parent surrogate, (e) placement of the child in an LRE, (f) statement of an individual education plan indicating functioning levels and objectives, (g) nonbiased assessment of the child's language, and (h) the practice of confidentiality by

8

professionals (Hallahan & Cruickshank, 1973; Lewis & Doorlag, 2006; Myers & Hammill, 1976).

Individuals With Disabilities Act (IDEA)

IDEA amendments of 1997 significantly improved the educational opportunities for children with disabilities. IDEA '97 additionally focuses on teaching and learning, and establishing high expectations for children with disabilities to achieve real educational results. IDEA changed from a law that merely provided children with disabilities access to an education to a law that provides improved opportunities for achievement results in areas of academia for all children in the U.S. educational system. IDEA '97 strengthens the role of parents in educational planning and decision making on behalf of their children. It focuses the students' educational planning process on promoting meaningful access to the general education curriculum.

IDEA has been revised many times over the years. Congress passed the most recent amendments in December 2004, with final regulations published in August 2006 (IDEA, 1997). The reauthorizations have reinforced the previous special education laws but have added the areas of autism, attention deficit disorder, and attention deficit/hyperactivity disorder as special education categories. There have been some changes within this reauthorization that look at how children are qualified to receive special education services. However, this dissertation study did not address these aspects of the reauthorization.

Statement of the Problem

It is not known how and to what extent puppetry may formally assist children with learning disabilities to improve their engagement and participation in class.

9

Additionally, it is not known how and to what extent puppetry as an instructional practice for educating children with learning disabilities within a holistic constructivist model impacts students' social and emotional growth. The study included data on the impact of socialization between the children with learning disabilities and their peers.

Because the current instructional practices are related to deficit-driven strategies, using a holistic constructivist modality may improve children's achievement academically and improve socialization with their nondisabled peers. Since the early 1970s, before P.L. 94-142 (Hallahan & Cruickshank, 1973; Hammill & Bartel, 1971), research indicated that the viable instructional approach with children with learning disabilities was to remediate their perceptual deficits. Lerner's (1971) textbook was organized solely around children's perceptual deficits in order to remediate their academic challenges so that they would achieve at the level of their peers. These deficits were diagnosed through specific assessments that were designated as effective protocols for children with learning disabilities (Haring & Bateman, 1977; Lerner, 1971).

The difficulty with the perceptual remediation techniques that were developed as curriculum and instructional strategies is that in the last three decades these instructional approaches have not made a significant impact in children's academic achievement. This has been reported by Heshusius (1989), Poplin (1988a, 1988b), and Poplin and Cousin (1996). This research is supported by Wiest and Kriel (1995), who stated specifically that parents and community are dissatisfied with the instruction that their children with learning disabilities are receiving. Therefore, based on the premise of the deficit-driven paradigm not being effective, which is the statement of the problem, this dissertation

10

investigated how and to what extent the use of puppetry contributed to the engagement, participation, and socialization between children with learning disabilities and their peers.

Purpose of the Study

The primary purpose of the study was to investigate how puppetry can be an effective instructional practice for children with learning disabilities to promote engagement and participation, and improve social and emotional well-being with their nondisabled peers. In addition, this research addressed research questions from a case study perspective by looking at the use of puppetry as a viable means for an instructional practice to promote engagement, participation, and social and emotional growth of children labeled as learning disabled. This qualitative dissertation, in the form of case study research, is defined by Bogdan and Biklen (2007) as "an attempt to understand the meaning of events and interactions of ordinary people in particular situations" (p. 25). Additionally, Creswell (2003) explained that case study is a qualitative method of research that is useful in investigating a complex issue and contributes additional knowledge to the already established body of research. Furthermore, according to Yin (1994), case study research focuses on detailed conceptual analysis that investigates a contemporary phenomenon within its real-life context.

Research Questions

The following research questions frame this qualitative study:

1. How and to what extent does the use of puppetry as holistic constructivist pedagogy for an instructional practice promote engagement and participation in children labeled as learning disabled?

11

2. How and to what extent does the use of puppetry as holistic constructivist pedagogy improve social and emotional growth for students labeled as learning disabled?

Research Sub-Questions

The following sub-questions were asked of the coresearchers. These questions focused the participants' attention on the aspects of puppetry as a reflection of their practice.

1. How do children respond emotionally after being exposed to puppets in a learning situation?

2. How do children with learning disabilities respond to the information presented by puppets that may show an understanding and acceptance of their disability?

3. How do students with learning disabilities incorporate information regarding academic, social, or emotional themes following a presentation by puppets from the Kids on the Block puppet troupe and other professional puppeteers in a learning situation?

Theoretical Framework

The following researchers contributed to the holistic constructivist theoretical framework for this dissertation. Piaget's (1952) research that related to observing children in the area of language development, dialogue, and play is an integral part of holistic constructivism. Additionally, the theory of constructivism addresses the work of Paulo Freire (1973). Liberatory education also includes additional research from Freire (1970), Freire and Macedo (1987), McLaren (1989), and Shor and Freire (1987). These theorists have interpreted the concepts of liberatory education synonymous with holistic constructivism, which is the theory that framed this dissertation as it has been applied from Freire's original 1970 research.

12

Liberatory education is an interactive process that defocuses on the teacher as the sole caretaker of knowledge (Freire, 1970). The recognition of the student as an active participant in their learning process is an essential element to the practice of the theories of liberatory education. As Freire explained in his seminal work, *Pedagogy of the Oppressed*, the current practices for classroom instruction is "the banking concept of education in which the scope of action allowed to the students extends only as far as receiving, filing and storing the deposits" (p. 58). Teachers are instructed to approach students as empty vessels with the responsibility of filling them with knowledge. Freire explained, "The teacher knows everything and the students know nothing, and the teacher talks and the students listen" (p. 59).

Liberatory educational theory is also based on the foundation of problem-posing concepts (McLaren, 1989). Students are given the responsibility to delve into subjects of personal concern. They can, for example, pose existing problems rather than having problems presented or dictated to them. The liberatory education concept says teachers are given the responsibility to introduce the students to a process—for instance, recycling. In this example, teachers ask students for ways to assist in solving the problem of ecological preservation. Students originate their personal concerns, which might revolve around a problem-posing concept of drinkable water. The students are given an opportunity to express their concern for the use of drinkable water. This process is liberatory because it originates from the students' perspective of their real-life experiences. Instead of being told what is important, they are sharing what is important in their life regarding their relationship within their environment. Hence, they are problem posing.

13

Additionally, the area of puppetry research by Kline, Stewart, and Murphy (2006), is discussed in this paper as a foundation for the framework that surrounds the theory of liberatory education. The theory base within the construct of puppetry is presented not only from an educational perspective but also social, emotional, and transformational perspectives for children with learning disabilities (Brown & Meeks, 1997). The use of puppetry as a three-dimensional mode of instruction (Peck & Virkler, 2006) relates strongly to Piaget's (1952) holistic constructivist theory.

Nature of the Study

The use of qualitative design from a case study perspective acknowledged personal awareness from the puppeteer's viewpoint. The individual interviews, researcher's observations, teacher feedback, students' evaluation of their experience with puppets guided the researcher in data analysis (Bogdan & Biklen, 2007) and investigated the use of puppetry as an instructional practice that resulted in an improved engagement, participation, and social and emotional growth of children labeled as learning disabled. These data collection methods were part of the process of triangulation of the data as described by Bogdan and Biklen. Additionally, whether or not the children's social emotional growth in the form of creating friendships and establishing acceptance among their peers and others improves their quality of life was explored.

Significance of the Study

The significance of the study through the qualitative methodology investigation was to learn whether the use of puppetry improves engagement, participation, and social, emotional relationships between learning disabled students and their peers. This

14

investigation was also significant because the area of puppetry as an instructional strategy for children with learning disabilities has limited research. This research is important if the study provides information that puppetry is an effective teaching tool to improve engagement, participation, and social skills of learning disabled students and nondisabled peers. The significance of investigating puppetry as an instructional strategy will assist teachers in the inclusion process for helping children with learning disabilities. Aspects of puppetry are entertainment driven with a participatory emphasis in which the child is an integral part of the process and a contributor to the curriculum via instructional design and delivery (Brown & Meeks, 1997). This study is significant to examine how puppetry can contribute as an instructional strategy for children with learning disabilities.

Definition of Terms

Banking education. Freire (1970) defined this as the practice of filling the minds of children with Information, similar to putting money in a savings account.

Case study. Hancock and Algozzine (2006) defined this as "identifying a topic that lends itself to in-depth analysis in a natural context using multiple sources of information" (p. 16).

Child find. Sorrells, Rieth, and Sindelar (2004) defined this as a process used to identify at-risk infants or toddlers under the age of 3 who would be at risk of experiencing a substantial developmental delay if early intervention services were not provided.

Deficit-driven. Poplin (1988a) defined this as any instructional program designed around students' inadequacies after diagnosing the particulars of an academic deficiency. In this approach, the deficiency becomes the focus of the teaching strategy.

15

Free and appropriate education (FAPE). Henley, Ramsey, and Algozzine (2002) defined this as "specially designed instruction, at no cost to parents, to meet the unique needs of the child with a disability" (p. 13).

Holistic constructivism. Poplin and Cousin (1996) defined this as instruction that includes offering students choices in meaningful tasks with authentic real-world experiences, providing whole texts centering around curricula on student experiences and knowledge.

Individualized education plan (IEP). Gorn (1997) defined this as a collaborative process between the parent and the school in which each child's educational program is developed. It is a written document containing all the essential components of a student's educational program.

Individuals With Disabilities Education Act (IDEA). Pierangelo (2003) defined this as the reauthorization of P.L. 94-142 in 1997. The law establishes procedures for any activity taking place in special education programs including assessment, identification, and IEP structure. Additionally, IDEA provides for the assurance of education for children with disabilities in the least restrictive environment.

Least restrictive environment (LRE). Ryndak and Alper (2003) defined this as the educational environment most like that of disabled children's nondisabled peers.

Liberatory pedagogy. Poplin and Cousin (1996) defined this as a way of using pedagogy to free students from the undue authority of texts and curriculum as well as cultural contexts so that they can gain new and more complex meanings from instruction. It may be used interchangeably with the term *holistic constructivism.*

16

No Child Left Behind (NCLB). Skrit, Harris, and Shriner (2005) defined this as the establishment of a set of basic academic standards that all students should achieve, holding schools accountable for meeting these standards and establishing teachers as highly qualified. Parents of students attending a failing school according to the adequate yearly progress (AYP) report will be given the choice to receive free tutoring or send their child to a different school.

Puppetry. Porshan (1980) defined this as a visual representation of people, animals, spirits, or deities related to a specific cultural. This visual representation can be in the form of puppets' appearance being simplified, distorted, or exaggerated.

Remediation. Lewis and Doorlag (2003) defined this "as the instructional approach that focuses on correcting the weaknesses of the student" (p. 445).

Specific learning disabilities.

> A severe discrepancy between achievement and intellectual ability in one or more of the areas, oral expression, listening comprehension, basic reading skill, reading comprehension, mathematical calculations, or mathematical reasoning. The child may not be identified as having a specific learning disability if the discrepancy between ability and achievement is primarily the result of visual, hearing, or motor handicap, mental retardation, emotional disturbance, or environmental, cultural, or economic disadvantage. (U.S. Office of Education, 1977, p. G1082)

Assumptions and Limitations

Assumptions

It was assumed that the puppet organization Kids on the Block had some knowledge from their performances that is related to educational progress of the students. The teachers had some understanding of how puppetry is related to their students' engagement, participation, and social and emotional progress. Another assumption was

17

that aspects of puppetry do influence children's engagement, participation, and social and emotional progress. The information gathered from the teacher interviews and interviews of the organization Kids on the Block, and other puppeteers, may be generalized to other instructional activities that use puppetry with children.

Limitations

The study was limited to the Kids on the Block puppetry organization and other puppeteers because they are the groups that originated the use of puppets to assist nondisabled children in helping to understand children with handicapping conditions. Another limitation in the research was that the special education teachers participating as coresearchers in the interviewing process were interacting with children with learning disabilities, although they may also teach children with other disabilities such as behavior disordered and mental retardation. The study was limited to investigating the group of children who qualify by the formal federal definition of children with learning disabilities.

CHAPTER 2. LITERATURE REVIEW

This literature review addresses how special education has changed from a deficit-driven practice to a more liberatory perspective. The literature discussed a movement for more liberatory education in the area of multiple intelligences as it applies to Freirean philosophy. An introduction of puppetry as a new liberatory approach and a viable instructional practice to help children enhance their intellectual, social, and emotional growth was examined in this literature review.

The first topic discussed is the history of the Education for All Handicapped Children Act of 1975 (P.L. 94-142). Prior to Congress enacting this law, children with special needs were not educated within the public school system. According to NICHCY (2004), in 1798, Congress passed a law to assist Naval personnel who were designated to have a disability or an illness with services; this law eventually became an extension of the current public health service. In addition to the history of P.L. 94-142, the reauthorization of the law under IDEA to a nondeficit or liberatory education model (Freire, 1970), addressing the need for multiple intelligences (Gardner, 1993) to serve as an instructional practice, is reviewed. Next, what learning disabilities are, how children with learning disabilities are they are classified, and what kind of instructional practices are relevant to learning disabilities are discussed. The last topic area relevant to this study is on puppetry as a creative practice for improving engagement, participation, and social and emotional success of children with learning disabilities.

19

History of the Special Education Law

The Medical Model

Legalizing support for individuals with special needs, according to NICHCY (2004), began with the passage in 1798 of a law that sanctioned a hospital to provide services to military personnel who were experiencing physical or mental life-altering situations that resulted in a diagnosis of a disability. That legislation was the impetus for the establishment of the public health service. The purpose in this designation as reported by NICHCY was to justify the need of medical intervention for military personnel. Continuing in the direction of the medical model, Wolfensberger (2003) discussed how institutions were created for persons with mental disabilities. Some of the citizens, as Wolfensberger explained, needed guardianship to protect their rights as human beings.

The term *normalization* as Wolfensberger (2003) discussed is grounded in the theory that people with disabilities are not normal but rather seen as abnormal and stereotyped by society within a medical model structure. This occurred because of the social mindset of society at that time. These practices became the impetus of the development and enactment of Public Law 94-142, the Education for All Handicapped Children Act of 1975.

The Enactment of Education for All Handicapped Children Act

As explained in Lewis and Doorlag (2003), there are seven tenets that are specific to the legal rights of children with special needs. First, every child with special education needs is guaranteed a free and appropriate public education. Second, each child with a disability has a right to be assessed without the discrimination of race, ethnicity, or disability. The third tenet acknowledges, after the child has been tested, the IEP team's obligation to develop an individualized educational plan (program). An IEP, as explained by Schuster (1985), is a written document that outlines goals and objectives appropriate to increase academic achievement within a modified curriculum. The IEP is a legal document that specifies classroom placement that is least restrictive, describes other services that are available to the child inside and outside the school environment, and identifies the type of disability being addressed. The fourth tenet identifies students who are designated as needing special education services as being educated in the least restricted environment or taught with their regular education peers. Specifically, *least restrictive environment* means that children are integrated or mainstreamed in a classroom setting where they learn alongside their regular education peers. These children increase their socialization skills, and as a result of classroom modeling there is improved academic achievement. This integration limits the stigma that is usually a by-product of the segregation of children with special needs (Ysseldyke, Algozzine, & Thurlow, 2000).

The fifth tenet acknowledges the need and right of parental participation in the planning of their children's program. The sixth tenet asserts that when a discrepancy ensues, the parent and children have a right to due process to protect their rights under the law. The seventh tenet is the obligation of the federal government to provide funding to the state to help in educating the children with special needs. Ysseldyke et al. (2000) confirmed the seven regulations, explaining that these provisions needed to be recognized and validated by school officials to better serve children with disabilities. Ysseldyke et al. also added information regarding the financial remuneration from the federal government that became part of the identification of children with special needs.

21

In relation to the tenets of the law as described previously, Briseno (2001) cited statistics that indicated more than 8 million children in the United States were identified as needing special education services. She also stated that prior to the law, because there was no identification, the needs of handicapped children were not being met. This information is supported by Lewis and Doorlag (2006) in reference to the inappropriateness of meeting the needs of children with disabilities. Categorizing children who were culturally or linguistically different, such as African Americans and Hispanics, who were significantly misrepresented, was the norm at the beginning of the establishment of the law. Ysseldyke et al. (2000) verified this information while discussing issues related to parental involvement. They stated that parents' concerns were generally ignored, and there was a lack of cooperation with parents of general education students. The main aspect that is recognized from Lewis and Doorlag, Briseno, and Ysseldyke et al. is that teachers and administrators forget to focus on children's right for a free and appropriate education with their peers.

With the establishment of P.L. 94-142 and the congregation and collaboration of parents of children with special needs, there was a movement away from segregating children with disabilities. Parents were starting to take a stand to ensure their children were getting the proper education that now had legal ramifications (Lewis & Doorlag, 2006). As a result of this as specified by Lewis and Doorlag, parents' contribution to the IEP process enables the IEP team to create a document that addresses the complete needs of the children with disabilities. Therefore, including the parent as a writer of goals and objectives to address their children's academic needs reinforces the importance of recognizing the parent as a stakeholder in their children's education.

IDEA, a Reenactment of P.L. 94-142

The acronym *IDEA* stands for Individuals With Disabilities Education Act. Since 1975, according to NICHCY (2004), there was a need to integrate changes that became amendments to the original law. A major provision under IDEA is the requirement as specified by Mueller, Singer, and Grace (2004) "that parents must be included in all the educational decisions of their children, including class placements" (p. 233). The 2004 provision of IDEA places the parent at the center of the IEP meeting, whereby they must participate in the IEP meeting and be asked specifically for how they want goals and objectives to be stated (Mueller et al.). This specific requirement for parental involvement has become noteworthy in 2004, as opposed to the original P.L. 94-142, that just specified that parents were part of the process in the development of the IEP and the implementation of the assessment plan (Lewis & Doorlag, 2006).

Another part of IDEA that is a carryover from P.L. 94-142 is the procedure of due process (Lewis & Doorlag, 2006; Lerner, 1971; Mueller et al., 2004; U.S. Department of Education, 2006). The United Nations Children's Fund (UNICEF) (2002) is at the forefront of providing parents a legal avenue for resolving disagreements or disputes within the IEP process. This due process is reciprocal as school districts also have a right to legally disagree with parents' decisions. Therefore, there is reciprocity in the law that was instituted in 1975 to protect both the parents' rights and the school district's rights for the educational benefit of the child being considered.

Reauthorization of IDEA

In the year 1997, Congress passed IDEA. The law was the impetus to provide fair and quality educational programs for children with disabilities. The focus of IDEA centers around three areas. The first area of teaching and learning emphasizes how academic achievement is obtained. The second area of parental support in planning and decision making of the IEP document is clarified. The third area focuses on securing meaningful access to the general education curriculum.

Liberatory Education

Traditional education as Shor and Freire (1987) discussed follows a structured standard that involves the teacher as an authority on curriculum, behavior, and process for learning. The teacher is seen as the knowledge base that children are to emulate and learn conceptionally from about subjects and content. A new paradigm, as Thomas Kuhn (1970) explained, must be implemented whereby children are not passive learners and both teachers and students can teach and learn. The present structure as Shor and Freire described is related to social authority. The format of schooling where the teacher is at the front of the classroom and the students are taking notes, following directions, staying on task, and completing the assignment reflects the present-day structural format of the classroom, school, and educators. Even though children are involved in discussions, as McLaren (1989) reiterated, student participation is still a passive act because their ideas and opinions are not valued. Shor and Freire (1987) explained "it is the teaching model most compatible with promoting the dominant authority in society and with disempowering students" (p. 10.)

In order for this paradigm to change, the format and structure of the educational system must take a radical turn. As Freire and Macedo (1987) described the radical movement, they expressed a process of "the notion of an emancipator literacy" (p. 198). Literacy is not just the process of learning to read but also the process of understanding

24

the world in which one lives (Freire, 1970). Therefore, the concept of emancipator literacy is really the contribution that the students make from their experiences, culture, background, ability to relate to others, and personal thoughts of their lived experiences (Giroux, 1988a). To be specific, the word *language* used in the context of this literature review refers to the children's language of life experiences rather than the language of communication. The language of communication that this literature review refers to is spoken English.

Freire and Macedo (1987) detailed how the struggle to change is representative of liberating human beings from a traditional set of beliefs to an understanding that with an acceptance of self comes liberation. They explain the importance of people accepting their own personal contribution to recreate the society. With people's ability to accept their knowledge base, the shift in the paradigm is tantamount to liberating education. Related to these concepts, McLaren (1989) stressed the need for Freire's (1970) concept of praxis as liberation for people. In other words, when people use the practice of dialectic communication, they are reflecting on their life experiences and putting those experiences into action, exhibiting that they have learned the concept of "reading the world" (Freire & Macedo, 1987 p. 1). McLaren emphasized that migrant workers transform as they learn to read the world.

McLaren's (1989) work stresses that Freire and Macedo's (1987) phrase "reading the world" (p. 1) has political ramifications because, as McLaren explained, of the need to "exercise the right to participate consciously in the sociohistorical transformation of their society" (p. 195). As a part of the application, within the school context of liberating education, Freire (1970) discussed that an acquisition of knowledge is not the

25

transmission of information. He coined the phrase "banking education…to refer to depositing knowledge rather than an interdependency of knowledge base" (p. 68). In contrast to the banking practice, Freire introduced "problem posing education" (p. 71) as a means for dialectic communication, which also becomes a true praxis. Under these conditions, people or students in school can be recognized as authentic in their engagement of knowledge because their ability to question and think creatively results in their authentic self. Problem posing is in support of Getzels and Csikszentmihalyi's (1976) research of art students who were asked to pose a question and then solve the question artistically. This research leads to a new concept of solving problems by first introducing students to the concept of posing problems.

Within this framework of problem posing, the concept of praxis may be an interpretation of pedagogy as Giroux (1988b) explained within the instructional practices of the curriculum. Giroux (1998b) continued to discuss that new connections to instructional practices must be introduced. The introduction of these practices relates more to the culture of the students than the curriculum itself. It becomes a framework of looking at the essence of instruction from the inside out. Freire (1970) interpreted this as "authentic liberation" (p. 66) in that it is the complete opposite of his banking education model. Students who participate in a liberatory education (Freire, 1970; Giroux, 1988a; McLaren, 1989; Shor & Freire, 1987) are actually practicing the concept of praxis. They use reflection as they dialogue about what is culturally important to them. The action part of praxis is their ability to read and then explain the topic of reflection. The critical pedagogies (Freire, 1970; Giroux, 1988b; McLaren, 1989; Shor & Freire, 1987) emphasize that dialectical interaction is not exclusively between the teacher and the

26

student. Students dialogue with one another. Shor and Freire explained this thinking as an intuitive exercise toward imagination. The process of using dialogue as an instructional practice establishes the basis for becoming critically literate.

McLaren reiterated in his 1989 work as he explained Freire's 1970 distinction of students who are critically literate, functionally literate, and culturally literate. It is important to distinguish between functional, cultural, and critical literacy because each represents a specific aspect of instruction based upon the experiences and background knowledge of each student. All three are needed for a well-rounded education, but each of them has distinctive practices in which each student will learn. All three are similar in the need to address each literacy within the design of the curriculum, but cultural literacy adds to an experience that is based on the social interaction of the student.

The pedagogy for liberation encompasses a framework involving three concepts of literacy. However, cultural literacy differs from critical and functional literacy in that cultural literacy accepts the totality of the students lived experiences within the society. Therefore, as Freire (1970) explained, before students can be critical, they have to embrace and share their lived experiences from a cultural context. He continued on, stating that the current situation in U.S. schools reflects the values relating to the technical aspects of curriculum and assumes that instructional practices are ideally the same with very little consideration for the culture or embracing the students' ability to be critical.

If these children are acknowledged for who they are as people and have the freedom to express themselves in a dialectical manner where there is equal exchange, they will experience and contribute to the transformation of society. More specifically,

27

Giroux (1988a) stated, "both mastery of specific skills and particular forms of knowledge literacy had to become a precondition for social and emotional emancipation" (p. 148).

Learning Disabilities

Because the purpose of this research study was to investigate children's curriculum in the special education area of learning disabilities, there was a need in this review of literature to discuss children with learning disabilities, how they are classified, and what kind of instructional practices are relevant. Therefore, this section covers areas of definition of learning disabilities, the concept of reductionism as a curriculum method, what curriculum and instructional strategies are most effective with learning disabilities as the literature emphasized and, finally, what general education teachers perceive as an effective mode, method, and practice in educating children with learning disabilities.

Before one can define the term *learning disabilities*, it is important, as explained by Keough (2005), to know how and why learning disabilities are classified. Keough explained that over the decades children have had difficulties with learning and academic achievements. Prior to 1975, there was no solid identification and, therefore, no classification for the children who are currently labeled as learning disabled. Hammill and Bartel (1971) reiterated the issue of no classification as they explained that the future of children with learning disabilities begins at the preschool level. For the purposes of classification, Hammill and Bartel recommended an identification of psychological deficits that relate to children's learning achievement to assist in the definition and classification. In addition to identifying and diagnosing children with specific learning disabilities, the process of intervention for remediating their deficits is an integral part of the instructional practice.

28

Keough (2005) stressed that the identification and classification of children with learning disabilities varies because individual educational systems do not use the same criteria. According to Myers and Hammill (1976), classification was not a new problem. There existed a practice of identifying children with learning disabilities as children with exceptional disabilities. Therefore, as Myers and Hammill explained, the term *exceptional children* was used synonymously with the term *specific learning disabilities*. They also explained that professionals in the field at that time did not agree on the taxonomy or semantics related to the field of learning disabilities. Some of the terms that were used at the time to identify a child with learning disabilities were *brain injured, minimal brain dysfunction,* and *educationally handicapped.* The terms *psychoneurological* and *learning disabilities* appeared at the time to narrow the scope for a more directed definition.

Warner and Sather-Bull (1986) approached the criteria of classification more specifically. They stated that a definition must come from a philosophical base and be related to educational curriculum design. Additionally, Warner and Sather-Bull specified that a definition of learning disabilities needs to identify children in such a way that teachers will be able to know which interventions are appropriate for their practice to address a child with learning disabilities. A definition of children with learning disabilities will then be operationalized by the teacher, who will disseminate the interventions within their own curriculum areas. Although a definition of learning disabilities was written in 1971 within the P.L. 94-142 framework, it is an outdated definition for the purpose of this literature review.

After the updating of the special education act, Pierangelo's (2003) definition is a restatement of IDEA to acknowledge reauthorization. Pierangelo defined *learning disabilities* as

> A disorder in one or more of the basic psychological processes in understanding or in using spoken or written language, which may manifest in imperfect ability to listen, think, speak, read, write, spell, or do mathematical equations. According to the law, learning disabilities do not include learning that problems that are primarily the result of visual, hearing, or motor disabilities; mental retardation; or environmental, cultural or economic disadvantage. (p. 268)

According to Myers and Hammill (1976), the definition by Pierangelo (2003) may not be a satisfactorily accurate definition. Myers and Hammill stated that the specifics of the definition include children served in special education. With this definition, some children would be placed in the classroom inappropriately because they had difficulty with listening, thinking, reading, writing, and spelling. For example, as Myers and Hammill specified, "in the Philadelphia public schools half of all the sixth grade population reads below the 17th percentile and surely they cannot all be learning disabled children" (p. 10). Warner and Sather-Bull (1986) stressed the importance of defining children with learning disabilities within an educational practical perspective rather than a psychosocial perspective. There is a distinct discrepancy between researchers Warner and Sather-Bull, and Myers and Hammill regarding the effectiveness of a definition for the children who have learning disabilities. Therefore, Pierangelo, and Warner and Sather-Bull agreed with Myers and Hammill's premise by reiterating that the definition of learning disabilities needs to originate in an educational foundation. However, as Myers and Hammill pointed out, the educational foundational definition still does not substantiate a definition that can be used globally, whereby educators can pinpoint which children really exhibit characteristics of learning disabilities as they are defined from an

30

educational perspective. That is the reason that Myers and Hammill preferred to use the clinical criteria that Warner and Sather-Bull opposed. Additionally, Keough's (2005) argument for understanding the definition and classification for learning disabilities originates from a deficit model. She stressed that children with learning disabilities are better served and supported through identifying processing deficits and using a system of interventions to assist the children with success.

Reductionism

The definition of *reductionism*, according to Poplin (1988a, p. 394), is the natural process by which skills are broken down into parts in an attempt to understand and learn concepts holistically. Although experts cannot agree on a solid definition for the term *learning disabilities*, there is an agreement that children with learning disabilities need to have curriculum strategies and content that remediate their specific disability in the content area of their academics. Warner and Sather-Bull (1986) explained that the process of remediation is related to direct instruction as an instructional strategy. They believe that direct instruction is a superior intervention for students with learning disabilities.

According to Poplin (1988a) and Heshusius (1986), the reductionistic paradigm is replete with mechanistic orientation of skills that teach the specific pieces related to each of the areas of subject matter, assuming those pieces will give the children the generalization of learning the content. For example, the reductionistic fallacy could be applied to the practice of children learning letters and sounds as they relate to the pronunciation of words. Many times, the children learn these letters and sounds but fail to apply them accurately for the pronunciation of words. Therefore, learning pieces and

31

reducing skills to individual concepts does not guarantee the result of learning words or pronunciation of the words. As Poplin explained, it is assumed that children who are not internalizing this reductionistic process just need more time and energy working with the same reductionistic strategies. Therefore, doing the same activity the same way for a longer period of time and expecting a different eventual result is the premise of reductionistic behavior. Forness (1988) supported Poplin's premise as he reiterated the failure of effective remedial strategies for academic curriculum to adequately assist children with learning disabilities.

As explained in textbooks that teach about children with learning disabilities, Lewis and Doorlag (2006) supported the reductionistic fallacy as they described a prescriptive model whereby every concept is broken down within a task analysis so that the children with learning disabilities will understand the concept and then be able to put the pieces of the task together as a whole. Kimball and Heron (1988) supported the reductionistic concept in their premise that students need to understand step-by-step procedures within the strategies that they are taught in order to understand and be problem solvers in their academic experience. They continued to reiterate that this process is systematic and does indeed build on previous learning.

The history of prescriptive teaching and task analysis, according to Wiederholt (1974), is dominated with well known educators. Wiederholt recognized Helmer Myklebust, Doris Johnson, Marianne Frostig, Samuel Kirk, Joseph Wepmen, and Grace Fernald as established theorists for prescriptive teaching of teaching children with learning disabilities. The prescriptive teaching from these historical researchers and theorists began through the use of diagnostic testing, which has it origins in the medical

32

model of diagnosis (Hirshelwood, 1917; Jackson, 1915). Poplin (1988a) reiterated the explanation of task analysis as the process of breaking down learning into smaller pieces so that the students will supposedly have an easier time understanding and generalizing the skill.

Because reductionism originates from the medical model, Wiederholt (1974) stated, the tendency has been to look at the process of remediation as something that the student must overcome. However, Poplin (1988a) stressed the concept of reductionism as a way to blame the student for their difficulties and behaviors. Student difficulties are critically examined through the use of behavior intervention strategies rather than focusing the attention on the student's ability to successfully complete the task. The concept explained by Warner and Sather-Bull (1986) specified that educational intervention is an aim of the teacher to assist the child in successful academic achievement.

Holistic Constructivism

The theories in holistic constructivism originated from Jean Piaget's (1952) work with his own children. He developed the theories of learning by watching his children play. These theories presented a new paradigm from the perspective of Thomas Kuhn's (1970) research, built on the need to view children with learning disabilities in a nondeficit model. The concepts of holism related to children with learning disabilities— as explained by Poplin (1988b), Heshusius (1989), and Hearne and Stone (1995)— present a new paradigm because the research identifies a need for change—not just reform, but a different view of teaching these type of students. The research is replete with reductionistic methods as continually explained by Myklebust (1968), Lerner

33

(1971), and Kuhn (1970), theorists that viewed children with learning disabilities as needing remediation. Their texts describe the various ways to remediate children's disabilities. However, a new genre of educators believes in tapping into the strengths and talents of children, therefore promoting an actual movement away from the reductionistic theory base to a holistic constructivist movement (Heshusius, 1989).

Thomas Kuhn (1970) defined *paradigm shift* as a movement or a shift in the way one knows and in a global or holistic set of assumptions that one embraces. The characteristics of a paradigm as Kuhn described include cohesion of a group toward a scientific discovery with emphasis on new open-ended problem-solving solutions, encouraging reexamination and rediscovery. Paradigms originated in the scientific realm, where research to understand scientific theory evolved. Many educational researchers view a paradigm shift as a reform and opportunity for trying new curriculum techniques. The difficulty with that view is that many reforms are only a different form of the same structure or approach. Consequently, when new curriculum is introduced, it is not really structurally different, but the difference is in format, organization, and sometimes information. Therefore, it is not truly a paradigm shift.

According to Jean Piaget (1954), each individual has their own spiral or learning curve. This process encompasses information that the learner gathers from life experiences. Knowledge is gained from personal experiences, associations, reading materials, and developmental milestones. Learning occurs within that context of past and present experiences as they relate to future happenings. These lived experiences are integrated as they transform or add to previous knowledge. Therefore, learning as an integration of past, present, and future knowledge means building on both new

34

knowledge and future knowledge by using previous knowledge and familiarity. The experience itself does not have value until there is reaction to it. When learning something new, the positive or negative experience will depend on incorporating the previous experience and knowledge.

Poplin (1988b) explained the principles of holistic constructivism, specifically identifying 12 concepts that are directly related to viewing not only a new model for teaching children with learning disabilities but also a new set of assumptions, or—as Thomas Kuhn (1970) stated—a new paradigm. Poplin is not explicit in her explanation and list of these principles regarding the order of importance.

Principle 1, the whole of the learned experience is greater than the sum of its parts, is a philosophical view of the Gestalt learning theories. One of the psychologists who stressed the Gestalt theory was Carl Jung (1970). He acknowledged the importance of integrating old information or meaning to assist in the learning of new information. This concept is supported by Freire (1970), who specified that children don't learn from "a banking education model, whereby they come to school as a blank slate" (p. 58). The ability to merge one's past experience with one's present knowledge forms a whole that is greater and much larger than the sum of the pieces, which are structured to have equal representation.

Principle number 2 specifies the interaction of the past and present experience as the impetus of the transformation of the individual's knowledge. Consequently, once new knowledge is acquired, the reflection of looking at the old knowledge is irrelevant.

Principle 3 states that learning is self-regulating and self-preserving. This principle refers to a protection that children have for themselves when they are placed in

35

compromising situations. Therefore, some children who are failing because of their learning disabilities stress their strengths or employ an avoidance technique, for example, becoming class clowns.

Principle 4 acknowledges that all human beings aggressively seek new understanding and learning as they construct new knowledge based on what they already know.

Principle 5 specifies that learning can be predicted through what the learner already knows. This concept is best described when teachers make a concerted effort to get to know the students in their classroom. For example, the sharing hour for children with learning disabilities who get to acknowledge their experience after visiting a sports museum becomes the impetus for sharing books on sports figures.

Principle 6 specifies that function and meaning come before accuracy. Again, this is related to the whole of the experience, which comes before the parts. To explain this principle, a noneducational example of seeing and tasting a cake comes before completing the ingredients in making the cake. Individual parts do not always guarantee that the child, especially the child with learning disabilities, is going to generalize those pieces to accurately construct a whole. However, if they view the whole first, they are more likely to see where the parts fit and, as a result, contribute to that whole. This example directly relates to the next principle, 7, which is in order to understand the concept of learning something—whether it be in the area of reading, math, history, or science—it is important to see it as a whole and then break the whole down to pieces to learn, rather than the reverse of learning the parts and making generalizations from the parts to the whole.

For example, when reading stories to children under the age of 4, there is no emphasis on teaching letters and letter sounds. Stories are read holistically to be shared and enjoyed. Questioning the child for comprehension of the story might be integrated into the process, but young children are not taught the specific letters or letter sounds before the reading of the story. This aspect of sharing story knowledge becomes informational and an integral part of the child's experience as they repeat familiar words and phrases and request the story to be read again and again.

Principle 7 states that individuals are better able to understand knowledge conceptually if they learn concepts globally, or as a whole. The individual parts and pieces of concepts can be learned after they understand the whole of the experience. Therefore, if individuals learn in this manner, the concept of generalization will be practiced effectively. For example, when learning the states and capitals, children learn that the states and capitals belong to the United States. The children understand the purpose and process of learning the capitals and states because they know their learning will result in the generalization of applying the knowledge holistically to the concept of what the United States means.

The next principle, 8, acknowledges the importance of errors. Learning is not effective or transformative without errors. Within the holistic constructivist teaching model, errors are acceptable as a learning tool. Therefore, instead of children's papers being marked in red ink to indicate the number and extent of the errors, there are procedures that teachers use to address the significance of an error and the acceptance of the children to change it. Errors are then seen as critical to learning.

The next principle, 9, establishes that for true learning to happen, the individual must be passionately involved. This is the justification for asking children about their passions and making their subject or curriculum area an integral part of the process. This does not negate the need for children to learn material that they are not passionate about, but if passion comes first, the result of their attention and focus may be more open for other subjects. The holistic constructivist principles originate from the child's perspective, who—as stated previously—moves from a passive learner to an active learner, resulting in a proactive learner/teacher/child rather than a reactive child.

The next principle, 10, may be associated with the experiences of life as a basis for how people really learn. Children who trust their teachers become more proactive learners. Trust comes from the authenticity, honesty, and integrity of the teacher.

The next holistic principle, 11, is related to Piaget's (1954) spiral of knowledge that identifies children's ability to generalize a concept based on their previous experience. These previous experiences begin with the interest of the child and expand that interest into new learning. This new learning is also by and large shared with others. The child takes pride in sharing personal knowledge and being recognized for that knowledge.

The last principle of holistic constructivism, 12, relates directly to the learning process. Children are honored for the integrity of what they know. Therefore, children do not have to be forced to learn, but they become teachers as well as learners and are acknowledged for what they share.

All 12 principles of holistic constructivism change the basic set of assumptions of the teaching and learning process. These principles also change the presentation of instruction as well as the development of curriculum and academic areas to be studied.

These principles truly acknowledge that the child is at the forefront of their education,

and what they know is truly embraced as a knowledge base to expand skill development.

Because this includes a reforming of values and beliefs of holistic constructivist teachers,

these principles can be acknowledged at the forefront of a paradigm shift in the field of

special education (Poplin, 1988b).

Curriculum and Instruction

Bryant (2003) discussed the perspective that effective intervention, especially at

the secondary level, has its origins in research-based practices. Students with learning

disabilities receive assistance in the areas of reading, comprehension, writing, and

vocabulary as a prerequisite for content area instruction. Similarly, Hammill and Bartell

(1971) viewed the concept of intervention to include programmed materials such as those

from SRA, Houghton Mifflin, Open Court, and Allyn and Bacon. Warner and Sather-Bull

(1986) supported the aspect of intervention; however, they saw it as a Band Aid approach

to the long-term effects of learning. Mercer and Mercer (2005) identified the need for

instructional processes to be universal so that all students can learn.

Kimball and Heron (1988) believed that teachers have a responsibility in

providing instruction to all children, but specified that children with learning disabilities

need a specified supervision of practice that relates directly to the application of

knowledge. They stressed that these concepts are very difficult for regular education

teachers who have children with learning disabilities participate in regular education

curriculum. Unlike the authors Kimball and Heron, and Mercer and Mercer (2005),

Stevens (1980) believed that few teachers are given appropriate knowledge about instruction that is practical for the child with learning disabilities to succeed. However, contrary to Steven's research, Keel, Dangel, and Owens (1999); Wiederholt (1974); and Lewis and Doorlag (2006) discussed in great length how the strategies of intervention in working with children with learning disabilities have been very successful and are still an acceptable practice. Keel et al. detailed how teacher-directed intervention within a system of step-by-step concepts and precision teaching allows the teacher to monitor their own instructional practices so that the child with learning disabilities receives the maximum effect of what is being taught.

These instructional practices are supported by Simmons, Kameenui, and Chard (1998), who discussed the importance of instructional practices specifically designed or tailored for children with learning disabilities. Simmons et al. also reiterated and supported the work of Bryant (2003) when they specified that an instructional practice for children with learning disabilities needs to have its foundation in theory and research. As classroom teachers accepting children in the mainstream, it is of utmost importance to understand the personal attitudes of general education classroom teachers as they relate to and teach children with learning disabilities (Lewis & Doorlag, 2006).

General Education Teachers' Beliefs

Teachers' beliefs, according to Jordan and Stavovich (2003), play a major role in how teachers devise instructional strategies that contribute to the success of children with learning disabilities in their classrooms. As Jordan and Stavovich explained, teachers see themselves as sensitive to the children so that they may engage them in classroom instruction that is accommodating for student success. Stevens (1980) acknowledged that there is a need for teacher to be a positive role model for the classroom because the children with learning disabilities in the general education environment tend to be teased and picked on. The teacher sets the example of acceptance and reassurance, critically stressing that the children's learning problems are not the children's fault. Jordan and Stavovich specified that successful teaching incorporate the best practices to be used for both children with learning disabilities and the general education students. The foundations for these practices originate from the teachers' perspectives and their belief systems of how they view children with learning disabilities mainstreamed in the regular classroom.

Jordan and Stavovich (2003) continued to stress the need for teachers to examine their own beliefs so that their practice will encompass positive approaches that will benefit all student success. Sometimes, teacher practices originate from their previous experience and knowledge they gained from university classes as they approach how children with learning disabilities experience learning compared with their peers in general education placements. Poplin and Cousin (1996) shared the view of teachers' beliefs with that of Jordan and Stavovich when they stated that inclusion or mainstreaming children from special education is both positive and negative as a result of the classroom teacher's beliefs. Poplin and Cousin stressed the need for the general education teacher to examine their attitudes and beliefs of children with learning disabilities in their classrooms. If the teachers have a positive attitude and an open belief about these children's potential, it will result in an effective learning environment.

Berry (2006) conducted a qualitative study about teachers' beliefs and used the writing process as the impetus for determining how teachers' beliefs contribute to actual instructional practice in the area of writing. The qualitative case study examined two

41

approaches to the writing process or writing instruction in an elementary school. The study did not propose to compare one writing instruction with another, but instead concentrated on the teachers' beliefs of executing the writing process and how their beliefs influenced the final outcomes of the study. In the study, Group A administered a writing curriculum practice within a structured writing format of process writing. Process writing included brainstorming, drafting, editing, rewriting, and publishing. Group B identified their writing as the writing workshop, which included a variety of different writing projects. These projects included response journals, mailbox, morning messages, response to reading, and a book club.

The children in both study groups included children with learning disabilities and general education students. The children with learning disabilities were integrated with their peers and participated fully with their peers. Both groups expressed a strong belief that their children should not be segregated for the activities. Additionally, Group B discussed the valuable contribution that the students with learning disabilities made to their learning community. There were definite similarities in the teachers' beliefs regardless of the teacher practices. According to Berry (2006), "students progress to become competent and self-directed communicators prepared for life beyond the classroom" (p. 21). Berry supported the tenet of student-directed learning by emphasizing that students are independent and learn how to cope with the demands of their learning environment.

Puppetry

Puppetry spans from the time of primitive storytelling, as explained by Kruger (2004), regarding folklore and stories passed from intergenerational knowledge.

Additionally, Kruger explained that primitive storytelling spans all cultures of the world as a way to communicate emotions, feelings, and indirectly impart knowledge. This section describes a historical perspective from the beginning of shadow puppetry with roots in Asia (Chen, 2002). The movement of expanding puppetry as an art form in Western civilization is discussed. This section also explores the acknowledgment of puppetry as a holistic constructivist style of education by Piaget (1954) and gives examples of how media and entertainment (Fowles & Voyat, 1974) have played a major part in the education of children through the use of puppetry. The section additionally describes how using the creative endeavors of puppets in the education world (i.e., the schools) can result in assisting children with learning disabilities to promote engagement, participation, and social and emotional growth.

Davis, Larkin, and Graves (2002) reiterated the importance of using puppets to engage the puppeteer and the audience. They explained that puppets have been acknowledged by Lesser (1974) in teaching and engaging children and adults within an interdependency mode. Consequently, both children and adults are exposed to problems that are posed in life experiences such as lack of self-concept or low self-esteem. As they watch the puppets interact, they recognize the puppets' abilities to show how positive self-concept can be experienced. Another example of interdependency is the teachings that are shared between the puppets as they interact with the audience. Through the mode of entertainment, this interaction becomes a lesson in character that is received by the audience of children. Lowe and Mathew (2000) supported this example in their statement "puppets encourage children to try out ideas and investigate their own" (p. 41).

Historical Perspective

Chen (2003) explained how shadow puppetry, the first form of puppetry, originated in China during the time of the Emperor between 140–86 BCE. The Emperor was a member of the Han Dynasty. The stories differ in exact detail, as explained by Chen, because there was no written record of the beginning of the art form related to the cultures. However, Chen explained that shadow puppetry was a part of the Indian culture, Chinese culture, Indonesian culture, and Cambodian, Thailand, and Malaysian cultures. Other areas of the world such as Turkey and Egypt were also recognized by Chen to employ shadow puppetry. Zuljevic (2005) reiterated how culture and the use of puppets created a mystical power to help children improve their communication skills.

The use of puppets, as Kruger (2004) discussed, helps to acknowledge, share, and provide a foundation for the understanding of culture, generation of ideas, and support of individual inner strength. In Euro-Asian and African societies, puppetry was used as a ritual for understanding the behavior and emotions of individuals. Kruger recognized this as disseminated in the theatre. Zuljevic (2005) discussed that the earliest puppets were ceremonial. Shamans used puppets as a way to acknowledge their power so that the people of the culture would show respect and believe in their healing powers. This was conducted as rituals for individual cultures.

Using puppetry as an art form for reflecting life experiences can be related to Poplin's (1988b) view of holistic constructivism, Gardner's (1993) theory of multiple intelligences, and Whitehead's (1978) theory of creativity. These theorists recognized that using puppetry as a form of recognizing children's voices would help them acknowledge and understand their own strengths and weaknesses. As a creative venue

44

from Whitehead's perspectives, puppetry can be seen as an entity for understanding life force. Whitehead's premise is that creativity encompasses both the universal principles of creation and humanity—that is, principles of self-creation. The introduction of puppetry within the field of education parallels Whitehead's principles of self-creation because puppetry as an art form promotes the social skills to understand children's emotional demeanor through social drama (Gronna, Serna, Kennedy, & Prater, 1999).

Shadow puppetry is the precursor to today's use of puppetry in the media for educational and entertainment purposes. There has been tremendous change since the introduction of puppetry in the United States over the last 30 years. Brown and Meeks (1997) stated, "the 1934 Communications Act of the United States mandated that radio (and eventually television) broadcasters should provide programs in the public interest" (p. 31). Puppetry in entertainment in radio began with Edgar Bergen (Mazzarella Bros., 2001), who personified the character of Charlie McCarthy. Bergen was the first to introduce the concept of puppetry for media entertainment in the United States. In addition to Bergen, Burr Tillstrom—originator of *Kukla, Fran, and Ollie*—used his puppets to explore and explain societal issues of the era (Mazzarella Bros.). The transition from radio to television began in the early 1950s with the introduction of *Howdy Doody*.

With the introduction of puppetry in the world of television media, there was a new form of marketing created to introduce the field of merchandising. The Mazzarella Bros. (2001) presented vignettes of Paul Winchell, Shari Lewis, and Jim Henson of Muppet fame to establish a foundational setting for the expansion of the use of puppets not only to entertain but to also teach. With the emphasis to move from entertainment to

45

an educational venue, the creation in 1969 of *Sesame Street* began the era of introducing academic skills to preschoolers.

Several studies included Cagno and Shively (1973); Gronna et al. (1999); and Peck and Virkler (2006), who recognized the importance of puppetry as an instructional practice. In addition, Synovitz (1999) conducted research that recognized puppetry as an instructional practice in the classroom for teaching academics, social skills, and preservice training for teachers. Research by Leyser (1984) acknowledged the versatility of puppets not only for use in instructional strategies but also in understanding and applying different learning styles in the teaching process. As an active teaching tool, puppets can be used with any other material such as posters, maps, or visual arts to help children understand curriculum concepts.

Synovitz (1999) stressed the need to use puppetry as an instructional practice for preservice training of teacher workshops. Because the use of puppets is creative and covers multisensory approaches to learning as explained in Gardner's (1983) work, it is a viable technique to help counselors, nurses, and health educators as well as classroom and special education teachers interact effectively while teaching concepts. Kline et al. (2006) used *Sesame Street* as the example for teaching academic curriculum skills to preschoolers. They stressed the importance of working with children at risk for learning and the use of children's television as a medium to support the learning of basic skills. With the use of *Sesame Street* as an active stimulus (Fowles & Voyat, 1974; Lesser 1974), children become knowledgeable of academic material through their interaction as both learners and teachers. This concept is supported by Leyser (1984), who specifies, "puppetry promotes an atmosphere of relaxation and enjoyment in which children are encouraged to become active learners" (p. 3).

Fowles and Voyat (1974) shared the premise that parents and teachers need to acknowledge that interacting with their children helps them practice the teaching and learning process. This supports Poplin's (1988b) premise of holistic constructivist teaching practices. When the student becomes both the teacher and the learner, there is a transformation, as described by Freire (1970). This also is expressed in the use of praxis, as Freire explained—the process of reflection and action. An example of reflection using the manipulation of a puppet is a puppet as a mirror of the child who is having trouble academically or emotionally. Once the child relates to the reflection by the entertainment of the puppet, the action part of praxis is their change in an improved self-concept, academic practice, and peer relationships.

Gronna et al. (1999) targeted one preschool-aged, visually impaired child to learn how to interact with her peer group through the use of puppetry. The child watched the puppets greet and interact with one another. The child then was scored on the ability to greet and interact with her peer group before and during free play. The results of the study indicated there were direct learning and transferences of learning through the puppetry demonstrations. According to Gronna et al., children's responses increased from a baseline of 4% to an increase of 100% after watching the puppets. This study was supported by the practice of Sister Marilyn (1964), who found that the use of puppets in a first-grade class helped the child's self-confidence as they learned to speak English that was grammatically correct by recognizing the children's input to help the puppet speak accurately. They developed a greater self-confidence in paralleling their spoken English to that of the puppets.

Cagno and Shively's (1973) study measured children's responses and enthusiasm while they watched a television program that included animation, film, animal puppets, three-dimensional objects, music, and stories. The segment of puppetry was very stimulating to the preschoolers in this study. Segments that ranked high to the preschoolers were puppet skits of quiz shows; and puppets joining in exercise activities, narrating filmstrips, and singing. The segments that ranked low in Cagno and Shively's study were marionettes, finger puppets, and finger plays. For the puppetry segment, the mean ratio was 97.9. This verifies concentration and motivation of preschoolers to be engaged when watching puppets perform.

In addition to the studies, Brown (2004) discussed the functionality of the use of puppets in classroom instruction as it relates to character education, art education, and school and community collaboration. In Brown's study, the use of shadow puppets helped fourth- and fifth-graders understand the literature they were reading regarding character education. Brown was aware of using shadow puppets in the islands of the South Pacific whose performances supported art, character, and community-building, and believed that the introduction of puppets for her fourth- and fifth-graders would serve to assist them in understanding related concepts. Students created their own shadow puppets. A student narrator for the literature being studied worked simultaneously with the student puppeteers. Results of this qualitative analysis indicated that students in puppetry performances learned valuable lessons related to their moral character. Student performers were not the only recipients of that knowledge. The audience who watched

48

the performance also learned about honesty, loyalty, and kindness. Collectively, they learned together as a school community. As the students shared the literature through puppetry, there was an acknowledgment of hearing their voices. This is parallel to Poplin's (1988b) and Peck and Virkler's (2006) explanation of holistic constructivist principles. These principles, according to Whitehead (1978), are interdependent with the creative process.

The specifics of using puppetry in academics related to reading and literacy were described by Peck and Virkler (2006). The study indicated that as a result of requiring second-graders to script a puppet show, their oral reading and confidence improved, and they were more fluent in reading and comprehension. Scripting also helped them improve their oral expression in reading aloud. A similar study (Zuljevic, 2005) found that when children performed puppet plays using scripting and reader's theatre, their reading skills and vocabulary improved. Additionally, the children's self-confidence and communication skills showed explicit development. The findings indicated that the use of puppetry as an instructional practice helped both the performers (puppeteers) as well as the students as they learned the social-studies content that they were studying in the second grade. This study practiced the conceptual framework of Gardner's (1993) theory of multiple intelligences. Visual artistic creativity was used as well as spatial intelligence. In addition, bodily kinesthetic intelligence was practiced as a result of the movement of the puppets. Bodily kinesthetic is "the ability to use one's body in highly differentiated and skilled ways for expression as well as goal oriented purposes" (p. 206). Gardner recognized that performers as puppeteers are included in the group of people who have bodily kinesthetic intelligence.

49

Support for puppetry in instructional strategies was discussed by Leyser and Wood (1980), who elaborated on how puppetry bridges a relationship between student behavior and learning. The study used a capture-and-record activity recognizing the frequencies of student arguments and specific ways in which the teacher intervened. A puppet was used for an intervention strategy to lessen the number of times students argued each day and identify teacher's ability to problem solve. Additional procedures in the study involved instruction to children on how to make their own puppets. The purpose of the puppet show presented by the children was to introduce classroom problems and provide a platform for the interaction of students who were not involved in the presentation. The show also offered solutions to solve the behavior problems that were exhibited during classroom instruction. In the study, the teacher recorded how many arguments were presented during a 10-day period. Statistically, there was a 1.5 decrease in arguments per day, and a 0.3 decrease in teacher resolutions per day. The study showed that the practice of using puppetry as an alternative for problem solving was effective in spite of the fact that the study was not a rigorous one, as stated by Leyser and Wood (1980). They believed that the use of puppets helped demonstrate the flexibility of the role of the teacher in problem-solving behavior interventions.

The use of puppets for instructional purposes is also recognized in Palumbo's (1986) study, which presented a puppet play to demonstrate cooperative play and stories that were of particular concern to a group of special-needs children. Palumbo specifically acknowledged the process as puppet therapy for children who were profoundly handicapped. Supporting the use of puppetry in special education, Leyser (1984) presented a list of special-education assessment tools that use puppets directly as a

50

stimulus for interacting with the children who are being assessed. These assessments are used frequently to help children with learning disabilities. They include the Peabody Language Development Kits (Dunn, Horton, & Smith, 1986) and Developing Understanding of Self and Others (Dinkmeyer, 1970). The Peabody Language Development Kit presents language, vocabulary words, and concepts in an interactive mode as the children are being assessed. The puppet is seen as the facilitator of the assessment. Developing Understanding of Self and Others also provides puppets for facilitating the information in assessing children with special needs. The organization of Kids on the Block uses their puppets to help children with and without disabilities learn to respect individuals with disabilities. Because the puppet shows incorporate a question-and-answer segment, it might be considered a criterion-referenced assessment helping the children comprehend the show they are observing.

The use of puppets in special education classes offers four practices that are valuable to the academic, social, emotional, and spiritual development of the children. Leyser (1984) discussed using puppets to motivate children. Puppets have a special connection that helps children maintain their interest. They are used as an instructional tool to assist children to develop their thinking skills, and provide a creative foundation. Puppets also help teach socialization, as Smith (2005) described the process of using puppets in performance for conflict resolution and teaching empathy. The puppets role-play, as Smith described, and the audience interacts during the performance. The performance shows how using *I* statements helps children resolve conflicts. Smith also described a workshop that introduces theatre games with the puppets to teach children about empathy. Children guess at the puppets' emotion and may predict the puppets' feelings. Additionally, the games can help with peer relationships and promote friendships, thereby helping nonhandicapped children understand the advantage of having a special-needs child as a friend.

Puppets have been known to help both children and adults change attitudes about associating with special-needs children (Aiello, 1977). The results of Palumbo's (1986) study indicated that students showed improvement in the relationships with their classmates. Teachers acknowledged that students were more enthusiastic and became less impatient after viewing the lesson that was taught by the puppets. Another result that transformed the class indicated that 3 out of 12 students took more initiative to speak and participate in aspects of the curriculum. There was also an emotional bond that was created between the special-needs students, who were puppeteers, and the administrators who served in that same role. A change in the behavior of children with special needs was observed after the puppet presentation. Both faculty and students made a transformation of more openness and supportive comments.

Palumbo (1986) stated emphatically, "Through puppetry and a therapeutic intent, we found that profoundly handicapped children could be helped to learn new personal and social skills" (p. 16). Leyser and Wood (1980) supported Palumbo's premise that puppets are valuable in helping children from a therapy perspective. Leyser and Wood stressed the practice by counselors, speech clinicians, doctors, and other health professionals who use puppets to help children express emotional trauma or any discomfort they may be experiencing. Bernier (2005) reiterated the importance of the symbolic roles that puppets play. For instance, "the police officer puppet can be a metaphor for parental authority, while the lost puppy may be symbolic of the child" (p.

129). The applications of these concepts are of primary importance when helping children deal with emotional frustration or unpleasant experiences. Puppets, in fact, are an integral part of the legal system to help children who are victims of abuse share their experiences in a nonthreatening way. Davis et al. (2002) stated that puppets can be used "to say or ask things that are unacceptable in other circumstances" (p. 47).

Summary

This literature has encompassed a movement from the deficit-driven model of special education toward a more holistic constructivist approach to instructional practices. From a new perspective of using puppetry as an instructional practice, the literature examined how puppetry can be used within the conceptual framework of holistic constructivism. The field of learning disabilities needs to move to a more liberatory (Shor & Freire, 1987) educational practice that includes an understanding of Kuhn's (1970) description of a new paradigm. The literature stressed the importance of changing the current practice from remediation to positive instructional supports in the mode of puppetry. Research has indicated that the use of puppetry can become more than a venue for entertainment, and can assist children with achieving academically and socially.

CHAPTER 3. METHODOLOGY

Chapter 3 discusses the research methodology related to case study. This chapter includes the statement of the research question, and lists the sub-questions that were asked of the participants. Also included in this chapter are the theoretical framework, researcher's philosophy, research design strategy, and research questions. Additionally, this chapter includes sampling design, a description of the participants, and a description of the setting. Data collection, data analysis, and ethical considerations are also described.

Theoretical Framework

Case study methodology was chosen as a research design from qualitative methodology. The research question, "How does the use of puppetry as an instructional alternative promote engagement, participation, and social and emotional growth of children labeled as learning disabled?", was directed within a case study definition. A case study is formally defined, according to Stake (1995), as a study in which the researcher investigates one or more participants through a process, activity, program, or event to gain an in-depth perspective from the point of view of the participants.

The research question addressed a specific group of children (i.e., children with learning disabilities) while simultaneously exploring through the interview process how an organization or a group of professional puppeteers, Kids on the Block, might help to transform the social and emotional development of this group of children. Additionally, the research investigation included 4 teachers who are presently teaching children with learning disabilities. Their perspective of how puppetry assists children's engagement, participation, and social and emotional development was examined. This study supported Becker's (1968) definition of the purpose of a case study. Becker specified acknowledging the group to be studied and a need for interaction between groups, and further explained the purpose of a case study within the context of how the research is related on a global perspective.

Researcher's Philosophy

Historically, the field of learning disabilities has been reductionistic. The mode of instructional practice has supported reductionism (Poplin & Stone, 1992). Children's television began with the premise to entertain and advocate diversity. With the advent in 1969 of *Sesame Street*, a new objective was introduced—to educate the child watching television. With the development of additional educational programs, there was still a lack in sound educational practices for children with learning disabilities. However, with the introduction of Kids on the Block (KOB) and other professional puppet presentations in 1977, a new era of educational supports were introduced.

These educational supports were presented to assist both children with learning disabilities and their nondisabled peers. Support in the form of a puppetry troupe was to help children become socially accepted while understanding limitations and positive attributes of children with disabilities. The philosophy of this researcher, after decades of teaching children with special education needs, acknowledges the need to investigate how a holistic constructivist mode of instruction might result in an increase in engagement and participation, and improved social skills between children with learning disabilities and their peers (Poplin, 1988a).

The use of puppetry as an instructional strategy may be a viable educational tool for the transformation of children with special needs, especially those with learning disabilities. Additionally, this researcher believes that the use of puppetry might be a vital educational instructional tool instead of just a mode of entertaining young children. The investigation of the use of puppetry offered a direction more toward holistic teaching approaches.

Research Design Strategy

The following research question, "How does the use of puppetry as an instructional model promote engagement, participation, and social and emotional growth of children labeled as learning disabled?", supported a case study design for the investigation of the particular group of students with special needs. Case study research, as explained by Hancock and Algozzine (2006), has three tenets specific to the design of the research, as verified by Stake (1995). First, it addresses a case or phenomenon to be investigated in the form of a situation, program, or activity. Second, a case study setting is in the natural surroundings where the particular case resides. Third, "case study research is richly descriptive, because it is grounded in deep and varied sources of information" (Hancock & Algozzine, 2006, p. 16). As Bogdan and Biklen (2007) explained, such information includes documents, handouts, and storyboards that are relevant to performance and feedback. This information is included in the case study along with personal researcher's field notes to assist the researcher in the process of triangulation. Using multiple data is supported by Hancock and Algozzine, who stated "doing case study research means identifying a topic that lends itself to in-depth analysis in a natural context using multiple sources of information" (p. 16)

56

Historical and current researchers in the study of qualitative methods and design consistently support this abbreviated definition. Additionally, the rationale and circumstances for conducting a case study transcend the historical as well as current knowledge base in the explanation of the components of a case study. Yin (1994) reiterated that a case study investigates real-life situations but adds that the real-life situations are investigated in a holistic and significant perspective, suggesting that the case has practical applications to assert the effectiveness of the end result of the study.

Merriam (2001) also explained one specific way a qualitative case study can be characterized: heuristic. The heuristic method is a guide holistically to investigate a problem (Merriam). As the teachers were interviewed in the present study, the researcher theorized that their explanations might lead to the discovery of new methodologies to be used with children with learning disabilities. The present study was designed to interview 9 coresearchers to address the effectiveness of puppetry as an appropriate instructional strategy for children labeled as learning disabled. This means, according to Merriam, that the investigation of this new instructional strategy constitutes new educational discoveries.

Research Questions

The following research questions frame this qualitative study:

1. How and to what extent does the use of puppetry as holistic constructivist pedagogy for an instructional practice promote engagement and participation in children labeled as learning disabled?

2. How and to what extent does the use of puppetry as holistic constructivist pedagogy improve social and emotional growth for students labeled as learning disabled?

The following sub-questions were asked of the coresearchers. These questions helped to focus the participant's attention on the aspects of puppetry as a reflection of their practice.

1. How do children respond emotionally after being exposed to puppets in a learning situation?

2. How do children with learning disabilities respond to the information presented by puppets that may show an understanding and acceptance of their disability?

3. How do students with learning disabilities incorporate information regarding academic, social, or emotional themes following a presentation by puppets from the Kids on the Block puppet troupe and other professional puppeteers in a learning situation?

Sampling Design/Description of Participants

The sample for this dissertation includes special education teachers from Stonebridge Academy (pseudonym) School District in Eureka (pseudonym), California, and puppeteers who belong to the Eureka chapter of Kids on the Block and other professional puppeteers.

Five teachers with 5 years or more teaching experience were chosen from the group of special education resource teachers from Stonebridge Academy School District. There were no other identifying criteria for choosing the teachers. A letter was written to invite them to participate in this study. The letter explained the purpose of the study and the significance. Letters were sent to 150 teachers, and the 5 teachers with all the necessary qualifications were chosen to participate in this case study.

The sample of 4 puppeteers from the Kids on the Block puppet troupe and other professional puppeteers in Eureka, California, were chosen from 30 puppeteers. A letter was given to all 30 puppeteers, and 4 individuals with all the necessary qualifications were chosen.

The study was delimited to experienced puppeteers from Kids on the Block or other professional organizations, and teachers with special education experience who exhibit innovative approaches for instruction.

Description of the Setting

The study included two specific settings. Two settings were described because there were two groups interviewed. All 5 teachers were interviewed away from the school at a location of their preference. The researcher was flexible with the time and location to interview each of the 5 teachers. For the subsequent interviews, the teachers' preferences were also honored. The second setting took place at the preferred environment of the professional puppeteers and the Kids on the Block puppeteers. The researcher traveled and arranged interview times on an individual basis for each of the coresearchers. The most important consideration was the area of comfort for all 9 coresearchers.

Data Collection

The data was collected similarly from both groups. For this research study, each participant (totaling 9 participants) received an introductory letter describing the study, purpose, and significance of this study. The letter also included a confidentiality agreement ensuring anonymity. Each participant was interviewed for a minimum of 1 hour, and each interview was tape-recorded. Permission for the tape-recording was obtained via the initial introductory letter. After each interview was recorded, each was transcribed from the tape-recording session.

Questions from the first interview that needed clarification were used as the impetus for each coresearcher's second interview. The researcher read the first tape-recorded sessions of each participant. Questions for the second and subsequent interviews evolved after reading the transcriptions from the first-session interviews. Each interviewed tape was marked with name of the participant and the time, day, and length of the interview. A separate audiotape was reserved for each participant. After all the first-session interviews were transcribed, the researcher read each transcription for each participant a minimum of three times. The reason for a minimum reading was to assess global tenets of each participant. Additionally, each reading produced questions that were asked for subsequent interviews.

Data collection also included field notes taken by the researcher. Any additional documents that were relevant to the data and the interview from the participants were collected. For example, documents included writing samples from the children (children's identities were protected). Additionally, data included a survey given to the children by either the puppet troupe or their teachers. All surveys were confidential. These documents were used to triangulate the data. The process of triangulation is used to verify and clarify the information collected from all sources of data (Bogdan & Biklen, 2007).

Field notes from each observation were included after each interview. The data was collected individually based on the results of each session. The researcher wrote observations to facilitate a continuous review of the data. Additionally, the researcher

60

compiled information in the form of short notes about the information that was being shared in order to assist in the data analysis (Merriam, 2001). The process of collecting information in various forms including interviews, documents, field notes, and personal memos/impressions is known as triangulation. The process of triangulation also included a peer reviewer who assisted in generating properties and categories, and verifying information from the transcriptions.

The researcher made contact with teachers from Stonebridge Academy to request their participation in this dissertation study. Additionally, the researcher initiated contact with Kids on the Block and other professional puppeteers via a telephone conversation to arrange meeting the members of the puppeteer troupe or group. Meeting the puppeteers for their voluntary participation in this study depended on their availability and time constraints. However, all those meeting the criterion of over 5 years as a puppeteer participated.

In this qualitative design case study, instruments included audiotaping and the transcription of each interview. Instrumentation also included documents or information that was helpful in addressing the research questions. This included any handouts from the puppeteer troupe and any follow-up worksheets that teachers distributed to the children before or after the puppet presentation. The researcher took field notes during and after each individual interview. These field notes acted as a support for the data being collected. The field notes included descriptions, impressions, and reflections of the individual during the interview. The multiple documents were used for triangulation.

Data Analysis

Data analysis begins with data collection (Merriam, 2001). As the transcriptions were read, keywords were identified in several transcriptions of the coresearchers. These words were underlined as they represented similarities of thoughts and perceptions among the coresearchers. To assist in analyzing, the data words and phrases of the coparticipants were represented by a color-coding process. The coding process was a physical representation and movement of coloring certain words, phrases, and patterns that appeared in several of the coresearchers' interviews. The issues that arose were color-coded and designated with abbreviated terms. Because the coding process is an evolving procedure (Bogdan & Biklen, 2007; Merriam), data changed periodically.

After reading the transcriptions several times and comparing each participant's interview, themes emerged. In addition, notations were made in the form of abbreviations to identify these themes. As these themes emerged, some changed form and were more relevant than others. The researcher held the research questions at the forefront while identifying these themes.

As Bogdan and Biklen (2007) explained, the coding system is the process by which the researcher is looking for regularities and patterns. Some coding categories can evolve while data is being collected, which is why Merriam (2001) stressed the need to look at data collection simultaneously with data interpretation and analysis. Coding categories can be modified, changed, or discarded as they evolve (Bogdan & Biklen). Once the categories are identified due to several participants indicating the specific theme in their interviews, a definition of each category emerged. This definition originated directly from the coresearchers' transcriptions.

Subtopics or properties that relate to each theme also evolved from reading the transcriptions. The properties were defined as well. The coresearchers' dialogue was chosen from the transcriptions to assist in data analysis. Their dialogue is a direct support for the formation of the properties and categories. This dialogue chosen as support ranges from a couple of words to a whole paragraph.

Although this data analysis could be manipulated with a computer program, this researcher chose to physically handle the transcriptions, memos, and field notes manually. A peer reviewer was used to help in the process of triangulation for the validity of the research data. The peer reviewer independently analyzed the data extracting categories and properties, and compared the information with the researcher. Similarities found between the researcher and the peer reviewer supported the triangulation and validity of the data.

Ethical Considerations

The ethical issues of this study involved the confidentiality of the individuals being interviewed, a protection of the responses collected, and anonymity. Their names had separate coding and pseudonyms to ensure anonymity. As they were interviewed, their feelings for not addressing a possible sensitive issue were considered. Regarding ethics, the researcher was cognizant and sensitive to the information that the coresearchers shared. The names of the human subjects were submitted to the Institutional Review Board but steps were taken to protect and safeguard the identity of the participants. A document granting permission for the coresearchers to participate in the study was submitted to the Institutional Review Board. The document specified that the human subjects could choose at any time to decline participation. The coresearchers

were aware that their identities were protected with the use of a pseudonym.

CHAPTER 4. DATA ANALYSIS AND RESULTS

This research addressed questions from a case study perspective by looking at the use of puppetry as a viable means for an instructional strategy to increase engagement, participation, and social and emotional growth of children labeled as learning disabled. This study examined how and to what extent puppetry is used as holistic constructivist pedagogy for an instructional strategy to promote engagement and participation of children labeled as learning disabled. Additionally, the study focused on how the use of puppetry as holistic constructivist pedagogy for instructional strategies assists the social and emotional growth of children labeled as learning disabled. Poplin (1988b) explained the principles of holistic constructivism, specifically identifying learning from the whole. The learning experience is greater than the sum of its parts. The theories related to Gestalt perspective result in a philosophical view of learning.

Data Collection

The collection and interpretation of the research data presented in this chapter consisted of audiotaping 9 participants (using pseudonyms), who are referred to as coresearchers in this chapter. Each participant was interviewed for an average of 1 hour in a location of their choice. Individual field notes were taken to support impressions of each interview. Each coresearcher was asked the following sub-questions: (a) How do students respond after being exposed to puppets in a learning situation?, (b) How do students with learning disabilities respond to the information presented by puppets that may show an understanding and acceptance of their disability?, and (c) How do students with learning disabilities incorporate information with a social or emotional theme following a presentation by puppets from Kids on the Block puppet troupe or other puppet presentations in a learning situation?

The first part of data collection was to transcribe all of the audiotaped interviews. Categories and properties from the interviews evolved by reading the transcriptions of each coresearcher a minimum of five times. During these readings, similarities of the coresearchers were designated to generate properties and categories. Keywords were underlined that described or explained key themes. The development of these themes resulted in identifying which themes were global and which were subcategories of the dominant theme. Occasionally, a theme designated as a property became a category or a category designated became a property. Depending on the commonalities that were identified, both properties and categories evolved from the concepts of the data.

It was the responsibility of the researcher to delve into the responses of the coresearchers while asking the questions, "What is significant to this coresearcher?" and "What drives them to say this?" The researcher was guided by these questions to generate the properties and categories. Each theme was given a color code and a name, which resulted in the use of mnemonics as a representation for the title of each category and property. For instance, the category *essence of character* was abbreviated *EC* and color-coded red. This process was discussed in Bogdan and Biklen's (2007) text on qualitative research design. The next step in organizing the data involved arranging the properties under the categories. Each category was given a color, and each property was double–color coded to identify the properties that related to their specific categories. For instance, the property *understand and relate to a variety of personalities* (URVP) was color-coded red/blue to represent the category of essence of character, whose color was red. This process was an organizational procedure that eased the process of identifying which properties were related to which categories. Each additional property that related to that category contained the color red, as they supported the transcription quotes related to each dominant category.

Once the categories were identified, each received a definition. The specific definition evolved from the coresearchers' interview data. Once the categories and the properties were defined, each property had a transcription quote from the appropriate coresearchers to support the evolved properties and categories. These transcription quotes became the supporting data for the rationale of the developing properties and categories. Each of the categories then became a support for the research questions. These are discussed in the data analysis section of this chapter.

Table 1 is a summary of the data that evolved from the transcriptions, containing each category and its properties, and definitions for each.

Table 1. Categories and Properties

Category 1: Essence of Character (EC)

Definition: The ability to transcend concepts.

Property	Definition
Understand and relate to a variety of personalities (URVP)	Acknowledging one's individual voice
Errors are accepted (EAA)	Mistakes are welcomed for learning
An internal sense of knowing (AISK)	The connection that clicks for concern and feelings of others while becoming in tune with another dimension to learning

Category 2: Human Connections (HC)

Definition: The ability to have a neutral connection that overcomes the reluctance and stigma of having a disability

Property	Definition
Communication (C)	The ability to approach conversations for appropriate meaning of what is being talked about for mutual understanding
Real and make-believe (RAM)	Fostering and understanding of how fantasy leads to the development of effective communication

Category 3: Interactive Responses (IR)

Definition: The ability to be actively engaged for communicating in the learning processes

Property	Definition
Simplicity of understanding concepts (SUC)	The enthusiasm and motivation for learning
Sustained engagement (SE)	The focus of attention

Category 4: Promoting Creativity (PC)

Definition: Use of imagination that unfolds, allowing one to become whatever one wants

Property	Definition
Increasing dimensions of learning (IDL)	The process and practice of helping to connect imagination through the action of learning
Problem solving (PS)	Thinking out of the box

Table 1. Categories and Properties *(continued)*

Category 5: Sense of Freedom (SF)	
Definition: An acknowledgment of self that represents openness to overcome barriers to learning	

Property	Definition
Ongoing dialogue (OD)	The acquisition of language and becoming vocal leads to continuous interaction with others, resulting in learning
Promoting self-awareness (PSA)	Developing a different way of speaking layered with cooperation, respect, and an awareness of self

Data Analysis

Category 1

Research Question 1 was, "How and to what extent does the use of puppetry as holistic constructivist pedagogy promote engagement and participation for students labeled as learning disabled?"

This research question is supported by category 1, essence of character. When children are engaged, they understand that their voices are important to the learning process. In addition, the coresearchers found that students understand that mistakes are accepted and that the students know that they are in tune with the process of learning.

Research Question 2, "How and to what extent does the use of puppetry as holistic constructivist pedagogy, promote social and emotional growth in students labeled as learning disabled? ", is supported by category 1, essence of character.

The coresearchers verified that the students have an internal sense of knowing that there is concern and feeling for others, which relates to their social and emotional growth.

Table 2. Category 1: Essence of Character (EC)

Category definition: The ability to transcend concepts

Property: Understand and Relate to a Variety of Personalities (URVP)

Property definition: Acknowledging one's individual voice

Dolly: I gave her a voice, personality and it was very interesting. I made her have a personality so it became a personification.

LeAnn: There is something that is very basic about puppets that the children can relate to as opposed to speaking to adults.

Loretta: They use words that express how they are feeling. They are clapping and laughing and having a wonderful time, judging from their responses during the show. When the show is over, they always come up to the stage trying to touch the puppets.

Waylon: They can relate to the personality of the puppets and the voice is just part of it and they don't notice the voice being different. They are focused on the personality and the appearance.

Property: Errors Are Accepted (EAA)

Property definition: Mistakes are welcomed for learning

Loretta: Being able to understand when it was their turn to speak, timing, turn-taking, they all want to be first, they want to be number one. Puppets make mistakes in conversation and the kids point out the mistakes.

Willie: The kids would act out scenarios like taking turns using the puppets. I can say they foster learning and enhance learning in a way that I don't completely understand why. They seem to retain the information better.

Reba: They were not comfortable doing role-playing I am not comfortable doing them myself so I am uncomfortable having the children but guess how we learn, we learn by doing so I practicing how to have conversations that are socially appropriate and go up to someone and doing whatever like making very inappropriate comments so we had to learn how to have social greeting show to approach things appropriately and that's how using puppets was beneficial.

Patsy: They used them to act them out and it always ended up with a fight. The puppets would be smacking each other around. Like I said, it was an outlet for them to vent some problems.

Table 2. Category 1: Essence of Character (EC) *(continued)*

Property: An Internal Sense of Knowing (AISK)

Property definition: The connection that clicks for concern and feelings of others while becoming in tune with another dimension to learning

Bonnie: After the performance the kids kind of sit quietly but then something clicks and they began to talk. We then jump back into the scripts, then after the performance we ask specific questions like, "What did you learn about say autism today? Can you tell me something you remember?", and I will praise them. Some amaze you and their questions are really sophisticated like one child asks, "Is Chris going to be OK?", showing a lot of concern and feeling where before the show there was none.

LeAnn: They internalize the learning because of the puppet because when I am using the puppet they are responding to the puppet they remember they are in tune to whatever is being talked about for that day because the puppet is there.

Tammy: They listen and watch because of the puppet.

Analysis of Category 1

Category 1, essence of character, addresses and supports both Research Question 1, "How and to what extent does the use of puppetry as holistic constructivist pedagogy promote engagement and participation for students labeled as learning disabled?" and 2, "How and to what extent does the use of puppetry as holistic constructivist pedagogy promote social and emotional growth in students labeled as learning disabled?" The coresearchers stressed the importance of how children understand and relate to the various personalities of the puppets. Their interaction, according to the researchers, became an acknowledgment that these children could have a voice of their own. See Table 2 for coresearchers' dialogue that supports these questions.

Additionally, the coresearchers reported that the internal voices of the children were acknowledged as a result of interacting with the puppets. They internalized feelings and were totally engaged in relating with the puppets. One coresearcher specifically stated that children who responded to the puppets were in tune to whatever the puppets

71

were discussing. The coresearchers also stressed the importance of the mistakes and how these mistakes can foster and enhance learning.

The need for the children to understand that errors are a part of life, and for them to internally know that they are whole even with a disability, transcends the essence of who they are. When the children become comfortable to speak up, their interaction with the puppets encourages their individual voice. One coresearcher discussed the importance of the children sitting quietly after the performance was over for time to reflect. Based on that time of reflection, many sophisticated questions resulted. Therefore, the coresearchers recognized the children's essence of character, because they were very engaged and willingly participated in the process of relating to the puppets. The coresearchers could feel their emotional and social connection to the puppets; in fact, many children opened up to the puppets before they would feel comfortable opening up to the adults.

Category 2

Research Question 1, which investigated student engagement and student participation of children with learning disabilities, supports category 2, human connections. The coresearchers stressed student participation and engagement when they shared the emphasis on conversations between the students and puppets that resulted in mutual understanding. Consequently, this mutual understanding leads to the students being more open about their disability and participating in class. Research Question 2, which investigated the social and emotional growth of children with learning disabilities, is also supported by category 2. The coresearchers emphasized the ability to be more comfortable and less stigmatized. This can relate to the social and emotional growth of

children with learning disabilities.

Table 3. Category 2: Human Connections (HC)

Category definition: The ability to have a neutral connection that overcomes the reluctance and stigma of having a disability

---

Property: Communication (C)

Property definition: The ability to approach conversations for appropriate meaning of what is being talked about for mutual understanding

Bonnie: After the performance, because there is so much enthusiasm that everyone has questions and wants to talk. After the performance the kids kind of sit quietly but then something clicks and they began to talk. How do the teachers react? They continue the conversation afterwards. They really jump in. They help to facilitate the language. They often ask about the puppets clothes or one has blue hair and they make connections to that when they say someone they know has hair like that or clothes like that. They make concrete observations and connections to real life.

LeAnn: Mostly for communication purposes. Mostly with communication because my kids were very reluctant to talk because of the stigma of having a[n] LD. They are afraid to speak up in certain situations.

Reba: Practicing fluency, that was a big help because they wouldn't be fluent with me one-on-one for some reason another object. The puppet was used to personify it. It was the puppet that brought out the language. That was really cool. There were many skills that could be tapped into.

Waylon: This will help in the communication piece. In nonviolent communication. To teach nonviolent ways. To communicate and act with people in a nonviolent manner.

Property: Real and Make-Believe (RAM)

Property definition: Fostering and understanding of how fantasy leads to the development of effective communication

Dolly: For skills, you are saying real and make-believe. To understand the difference in real and make-believe for the younger students by pointing out that animals really don't talk.

Loretta: It was an animal that could talk to the children. A talking animal. What a fantasy. The kids liked that and honed in on that.

Waylon: I think kids can't distinguish reality and fantasy and the kids think they are real in some way and I think that may be what it is that is the fascination with the puppets. The connection to real life. They liked the venue. It was like a magic world for them. It was not like the world to them that they normally see walking down the street or in the supermarket.

Analysis of Category 2

Category 2, human connections, addresses and supports the research question related to student engagement and participation, as well as social and emotional growth. The coresearchers emphasized the importance of communication and distinction between real and make-believe to assist the children with overcoming the reluctance and stigma of having a disability. These two properties related strongly to human connections. Because the coresearchers believed that the students' communications with the puppets effectively helped them make the connections, those connections became the impetus for teaching them how to connect to the coresearchers. The puppets were used as a segue for opening communication and relationships to the coresearchers. See Table 3 for coresearchers' dialogue that supports the research question.

Because the Kids on the Block puppets were constructed to reflect real-life children with disabilities, even though they were not real, they were still sharing their experiences as characters with handicapping conditions. This acknowledgment helped the children make the connections to real life, even though the puppet presentation was like a "magic world," as one coresearcher said. The children were able to make the connection with themselves and the coresearchers that they could overcome the stigma of having a disability. This relationship between the puppets and the children showed a strong engagement, as the researchers explained that the puppets not only helped to foster children's connections to the real world but also helped the children see physical features as a connection to their own disability.

Inherent in category 2, human connections, is the improvement to children's engagement and participation as it relates to the research question. Because the

74

coresearchers helped the children to understand the difference between fantasy and reality, the children additionally projected a sense of social and emotional maturity.

Category 3

Research Question 1 on student engagement and participation of students with learning disabilities using puppetry as an instructional strategy was supported by category 3, interactive responses. The coresearchers commented on the students' motivation and enthusiasm for academic learning, which resulted in engagement and participation in instruction. They also emphasized that after a puppetry presentation, the students' attention was more focused on instruction. In fact, one coresearcher emphasized a decrease in behavior problems. Research Question 2 is not supported by category 3. Because the coresearchers emphasized learning and the students' focus of attention for category 3, there were no relationships to students' social or emotional growth.

Table 4. Category 3: Interactive Responses (IR)

Category definition: The ability to be actively engaged for communicating in the learning processes

Property: Simplicity of Understanding Concepts (SUC)

Property definition: The enthusiasm and motivation for learning

Reba: Used in social studies, writing, math, and science and they always seem to get more out of the lesson. Were used to generalize content in an effort to pull in and simplify everything. We can follow directions, which is literacy.

LeAnn: To extend and simplify learning. Asks what-to-do questions.

Willie: Having the puppet demonstrate the problem on the board. Augment the story.

Tammy: Beneficial to preschool teaching concepts. The lesson supports the teaching. Grabs their attention in teaching the harder concepts.

Patsy: Helps to remember the information in smaller units. The visual part helps the child remember. Used to demonstrate. Modify the vocabulary of the lesson to fit the specific children and keeps the whole thing in the third person. It is pretty basic. Mostly basic academic concepts were reinforced or taught.

Table 4. Category 3: Interactive Responses (IR) *(continued)*

Property: Simplicity of Understanding Concepts (SUC) *(continued)*

Dolly: Simple stories about using common sense and being clever.

Loretta: A puppet takes it to a different level by putting the kids automatically relax. You are more open when you are relaxed so then you don't have a threatening atmosphere and sometimes kids put up blocks but the puppets tear those offensives down. A puppet is not an authority figure and brings things down to a whole different level but you can still teach them the same information in a stress-free environment.

Property: Sustained Engagement (SE)

Property definition: The focus of attention

Dolly: To pay attention to the details. You learn their limits in attention while you are presenting a performance and you adjust to that instead of a specific audience. I think it is because of all the new technology kids have short attention spans and they get shorter and shorter but the puppets help to keep the kids engaged. We have had to adjust the shows to accommodate this.

LeAnn: It is nonthreatening and it gets their attention.

Loretta: Most kids fixated on the interactions of the puppet. My focus was totally on the puppet it was a precursor to, which captures the child's attention and imagination and keeps them focused. We have to create a story that keeps the audience['s] attention. Sheer attention and enthusiasm. Video, watch it over and over again, integrating technology. Within the classroom environment the kids are frustrated, resistant, unfocused until you incorporate puppets into the classroom and to support the curriculum.

Reba: To interact they really become actively engaged and attention is definitely much better.

Tammy: All the kids were paying attention while the puppet talked. It really grabs their attention.

Waylon: Use of voices to gain attention. The use of the voices was not an issue because the kids did not even recognize the voice. For the kids it didn't matter that the different voices [were] being used because they saw and [were] focused on the puppet and...being like this creature that was talking with them. They didn't care if there was a different voice. They saw the voice as being attached to the puppet and it was the one that doing the talking and [they] are focused on this thing talking to them. The puppets were interactive so the kids were totally focused on what was going on. Him saying something like, "Are you kids paying attention?" You don't focus on the person or the operator; you see the puppet.

Willie: There were no behavior problems because the kids were focused on the puppets.

Analysis of Category 3

Category 3, interactive responses, addresses and supports only Research Question 1, related to the promotion of engagement for children labeled as learning disabled within a holistic perspective. According to the coresearchers, children who are actively engaged

76

have the enthusiasm and motivation for learning. Therefore, the property of simplicity of understanding concepts and the property of sustained engagement focuses on the carryover of learning into academic subjects. See Table 4 for coresearchers' dialogue that supports Research Question 1.

The coresearchers explained that they use the puppets to demonstrate problems and concepts related to specific curriculum. The coresearchers stressed how the children paid close attention to learning the information and that the puppets seemed to simplify difficult concepts. For instance, one coresearcher said that using the puppets for social studies, writing, math, and science results in sustained recall. Another coresearcher discussed the advantage that puppets have as the children were focused on the learning and less resistant to outside disruptions. This interaction captured children's attention and imagination, and kept them focused.

The coresearchers stressed that participation and engagement, or the effort to focus the children's attention, was sustained for the duration of class time. Consequently, even though children may not have realized it, they were truly learning. This learning was evident because of the interaction the children had with the coresearchers. One coresearcher emphasized how the simplicity of understanding concepts related to the children's common sense and their ability to be clever. According to the coresearchers, the category of interactive responses was prevalent in the practice of lesson presentation. Children were engaged and focused. This substantiates the research question on improving engagement and participation. Because their learning also includes interaction in the classroom, their ability to participate was due in part to the relationship with the puppets.

77

Category 4

Research Question 1, which explored engagement and participation of children with learning disabilities using puppetry as an instructional strategy, is supported by the category 4, promoting creativity. The coresearchers emphasized the students' connection with their imagination as it related to the process and action of learning academic subjects. For instance, one coresearcher stated that the relationships and the puppet presentation spurred imagination and creativity, which extended the curriculum. The coresearchers also explained how the students were able to problem solve by thinking out of the box. Research Question 2, which examines the social and emotional growth of children with learning disabilities using puppetry as an instructional strategy, was not supported by category 4.

Table 5. Category 4: Promoting Creativity (PC)

Category definition: Use of imagination that unfolds, allowing one to become whatever one wants
Property: Increasing Dimensions of Learning (IDL)
Property definition: The process and practice of helping to connect imagination through the action of learning
Dolly: They get to design and use their own voice or give the puppet the voice.
LeAnn: They would mimic the same when they were allowed to use. They mimic what had been done.
Loretta: Spurs imagination and creativity. Extends the curriculum.
Patsy: They act out events. They created puppets that looked like something out of Stephen King movie. They were an extra visual aide for teaching and reteaching. Puppets mirror the right brain.
Reba: Combination of entertainment and other choices. Not a store-bought puppet but one they created. Kind of a visual of something that took place long ago. Acting out what I was talking about, they get to act out and do things. They created puppets with all kinds of disabilities.

Table 5. Category 4: Promoting Creativity (PC) *(continued)*

Property: Problem Solving (PS)

Property definition: Thinking out of the box

Dolly: Problem solving. Thinking out of the box to find another way around the problem which folds into the creativity aspect. It brings problem solving into focus, like how do you get a puppet through the window? You come out of your physical envelope.

LeAnn: The students would have to change their demeanor in social situations.

Waylon: It is an alternative to the standard practice. You can interject some stuff to extend the learning. It is another voice to hear, another thought process to hear, and another interactive process for the kids to get involved with. It is the same as dressing up as the character.

Analysis of Category 4

Category 4, promoting creativity, addresses only Research Question 1 on student engagement and participation of children with learning disabilities by using puppets as an instructional practice. This category specifically addresses and supports the conceptual framework of holistic constructivist methodology. Because the concept of creativity recognizes the global aspects of individuals, it acknowledges the process of constructing meaning through the use of puppetry. Supporting the concept of holistic constructivism, the coresearchers specified that the use of imagination in promoting creativity increases the dimensions of learning. Additionally, the coresearchers acknowledged that working with the puppets helped the children become problem solvers, thinking out of the box. See Table 5 for coresearchers' dialogue that supports Research Question 1.

One coresearcher stated the importance of allowing the children to create their own puppets and giving them a chance to act out scenarios based on creating their own voice for their particular puppet. That coresearcher helped them create puppets with all kinds of disabilities. Another coresearcher stressed the creativity of children changing their demeanor as they began to interact with the puppets. A consensus by the coresearchers establishes the practice of extending academic curriculum, and fostering imagination and creativity. Therefore, using puppets combines entertainment, creativity, and engagement in academic learning and social growth.

Category 5

Research Question 1, which investigated the student engagement and participation of children with learning disabilities by using puppetry as an instructional strategy, is supported by category 5, sense of freedom. The coresearchers explained that the students' sense of freedom resulted in their understanding that once they are engaged in the learning process, and are able to participate academically. The freedom to share information about their disability and acknowledge that it is acceptable to have a disability became the impetus for their freedom. Once they were free, they were more comfortable in engaging in instructional activities and participating with their peers. For example, two coresearchers stressed the importance of students learning to write their own scripts, which taught them not only about the writing process but also about puppeteering.

Research Question 2, which explored the social and emotional growth of children with learning disabilities by using puppetry as an instructional practice, is supported by category 5. The coresearchers explained how the experience of interacting with the puppets promoted the students' self-awareness related to cooperation and respect for others while also accepting one's self. One coresearcher explained one of her student's experience of self-acceptance and socializing with other children. When the puppet explained their experience with hemophilia, her student felt the freedom to share his experience because he had the same experience. Therefore, the engagement in

conversation led the other children in the class to be more empathetic to that child.

Table 6. Category 5: Sense of Freedom (SF)

Category definition: An acknowledgment of self that represents openness to overcome barriers to learning

Property: Ongoing Dialogue (OD)

Property definition: The acquisition of language and becoming vocal leads to continuous interaction with others, resulting in learning

Bonnie: Some amaze you and their questions are really sophisticated. They want to talk to him exclusively. That support we are all the same. Everybody seems to relate.

One of my experiences was, in Eureka we did a show because there was a student there who had hemophilia and he was reluctant to participate in virtually anything. He would not socialize with any of the other children. So I took the puppet that we had that was a representation of hemophilia [and] this was used to support the awareness of the disability. We did that one script and the child finally put his hand up and acknowledged that he has that, which began the conversation, and the puppet thanked him for sharing.

Dolly: I don't think the kids realize they are learning. They were used across the curriculum but mostly in the language arts, science, and social/emotional [social scripts for appropriate behavior). We would invite another classroom to come and watch. They discuss it for a long time after the show is over, then do more the next time.

LeAnn: Facilitate socialization skills and listening skills. It was cross-curriculum. I used them in all areas of instruction. There was a particular time of day when I used them to talk about socialization with other students in an appropriate manner. It was before lunch or after recess. How to be a friend, to take turns, and to be polite on the playground was emphasized. There were stories with morals and when Lilly is not there, they ask about her, wanting to know when Lilly is coming back. They look forward to her coming and they miss when she is not there and they remember the lesson better when she is there. I intend to do more now from the aspect of learning and supporting instruction. Use across the curriculum. Enhance my teaching and my ability to get the lessons across.

Reba: Writing dialogue. Many skills that could be tapped into like writing their own scripts. With all the kids from autism to LD to reverse mainstreaming and even general education kids.

Willie: Interact with the puppet and the story on their own and this went on all day when they had individual time. Students who were otherwise shy became very vocal. Begun to have students with autism and they seem to like.

Table 6. Category 5: Sense of Freedom (SF) *(continued)*

Property: Promoting Self-Awareness (PSA)

Property definition: Developing a different way of speaking layered with cooperation, respect, and an awareness of self

Bonnie: The child finally put his hand up and acknowledged that he has that, which began the conversation, and the puppet thanked him for sharing and then he was able to talk about his experiences with the doctors and the disability, then the other students showed marked interest in the child after the show. Everyone wanted to be his "friend." We discuss the topic of the disabilities. Shows add courage in speaking about their disability. Not to tease or make fun of a person with a disability. Was used to support the awareness of the disability.

Dolly: They also bring awareness to different cultures and ways of speaking. We also work in with socialization and cooperation with each other as well as using good manners and being helpful. We also stress turn-taking and being polite. Cooperation and sequencing. We teach beginning, middle, and end. We used *The Very Busy Spider,* that is, beginning to end, and I also like to work with respect because that is important to all even the respect of the spider because it took the spider all day to make the web. We want the kids to use respect in all areas that is included in the art of puppetry. We also bring awareness to gender issues and being one's self, and individual, not to go with the herd. In puppetry, a boy can play a girl, a girl can play a cow. You come out of your physical envelope.

LeAnn: I used this song to get the audience to begin to interact and respond to the puppet, kind of like a sing-along. With kids that were reluctant I would start the song and the kids would join in.

Loretta: We're all different, so we were fostering respect for diversity and as result we were teaching respect for disabilities. Like, they were real puppeteers and they had to be able to read and follow a written script being able to understand when it was their turn to speak. Timing, turn-taking, they all want to be first, they want to be number one. Kids write scripts for me to use. We give them ideas. We put the idea out there and let their imaginations run with it, so we really see a lot of collaboration with the students on a script, so we are actually teaching the kids to be puppeteers exactly. They come up with the story.

Analysis of Category 5

Category 5, sense of freedom, substantiates both Research Question 1, which asks

how and to what extent does the use of puppetry as a holistic constructivist pedagogy for

an instructional strategy promote the engagement and participation of children labeled as

learning disabled, and 2, which asks how and to what extent does the use of puppetry as a

holistic constructivist pedagogy for an instructional strategy promote social and emotional growth in children labeled as learning disabled. See Table 6 for coresearchers' dialogue that supports the research questions.

The coresearchers identified the property of ongoing dialogue and the property of promoting self-awareness as support for the concept of freedom. They explained that when the children interact with the puppets, it facilitated socialization, listening, and self-awareness. These concepts represent children's ability to be free from frustration. The coresearchers explained there was an ongoing dialogue between the children and the puppets that eventually carried over to a speaking and writing dialogue in their classroom situation.

Freedom also entails the children's ability to interact not only with the puppets but also with other children and adults, and to be accepted in spite of their disability. One coresearcher stated that the children were taught how to be a friend, take turns, be polite on the playground, and have appropriate social conversations, which resulted in feeling free to speak without hesitation. The coresearchers stressed the concepts previously mentioned as beginning with the conservations with the puppets. Because the coresearchers emphasized conversations with the puppets as a first step, they acknowledged that this dialogue resulted in promoting self-awareness and self-acceptance. Two coresearchers reiterated that the property of self-awareness resulted in the understanding and fostering respect for diversity, different cultures, and disabilities. One coresearcher supported that respect also included respect for gender.

Category 5, sense of freedom, represents openness to overcoming barriers to learning. Consequently, freedom involves an acknowledgment of self. There is flexibility as children interact with others; they know they can become whoever they want. The

83

coresearchers recognized that the puppets became an impetus for helping children with learning disabilities promote their own self-awareness, leading to an understanding that their learning becomes the foundation for their freedom. The category of sense of freedom relates to engagement and participation of the children who are labeled as learning disabled, as well as to helping them grow socially and emotionally.

Summary

The concepts that were presented through the ideas and dialogue of the coresearchers resulted in support of the holistic constructivist principles. The categories of essence of character, human connections, and sense of freedom presented a deep acknowledgment and understanding of how the use of puppetry as an instructional strategy is a successful method for helping children labeled as learning disabled become more engaged in their learning and more socially accepted. The coresearchers also acknowledged the use of puppetry helped the children with learning disabilities promote their own self-awareness for their disabilities, which resulted in being accepted by their peers. The puppets became, according to the coresearchers, an integral part of the children's progress and support of learning.

The categories of interactive responses and promoting creativity were recognized by the coresearchers as more hands-on and practical applications of using the puppets as an instructional strategy. The coresearchers stressed the interactive responses related to academic content, and the enthusiasm and motivation the children with learning disabilities had after experiencing the puppet shows. The coresearchers also shared the practical use of combining the entertainment of puppetry with education or problem solving techniques, which resulted in promoting creativity. By interacting with the puppets and participating in the puppet shows, the children were given an opportunity to understand how their imagination and voice for speaking about their disability could be developed. The coresearchers stressed the importance of the children's responses and emotional openness after watching the puppets, especially those puppets with disabilities. The coresearchers expressed how the children recognized their strengths and became more in tune with themselves and their ability to learn.

CHAPTER 5. SUMMARY, DISCUSSION, IMPLICATIONS, AND RECOMMENDATIONS

Summary

The primary purpose of the study investigated how puppetry can be an effective instructional strategy for children with learning disabilities to promote engagement and participation, and improve social and emotional well-being with their nondisabled peers. This qualitative dissertation was conducted in the form of case study research as defined by Bogdan and Biklen (2007). Creswell (2003) explained that case study is a qualitative method of research that is useful in investigating a complex issue, and contributes additional knowledge to the already established body of research. Two research questions guided the study: "How and to what extent does the use of puppetry as holistic constructivist pedagogy for an instructional strategy promote engagement and participation in children labeled as learning disabled?" and "How and to what extent does the use of puppetry as holistic constructivist pedagogy for an instructional strategy promote social and emotional growth in children labeled as learning disabled?"

The results of the data indicated five categories of significance that evolved from analyzing the transcriptions and identifying similarities within each of the coresearcher comments. The coresearcher participants included 5 special education teachers from Stonebridge Academy, and 4 puppeteers with 1 puppeteer associated with Kids on the Block and 3 other puppeteers familiar with puppet shows that relate to children with special education needs. The five categories included *essence of character, human* connections, *interactive responses, promoting creativity,* and *sense of freedom.* These categories evolved from reading the participants transcriptions a minimum of five times. This chapter is a culmination of how the categories from the current study relate to the research literature, and how the analysis leads to the implications for future research.

Discussion

The first category, essence of character, included the properties of *understanding and relating to a variety of personalities, errors are accepted,* and *an internal sense of knowing.* These properties related to an acknowledgment of how learning occurs. The participants were very emphatic on specifying the importance of acknowledging the voices of the children. The term *children* in this discussion refers to children with learning disabilities. There are several researchers who support the category of essence of character as well as the related properties.

Freire (1970) reported on the importance of acknowledging one's voice in the transformation of individuals. Freire also stated that the importance of giving voice to the illiterate people in his work in Brazil helped to reinforce the character of the Brazilian people. This can be directly related to the information presented by the coresearchers. The coresearchers specified the difficulty their children had as students with disabilities, and how the introduction of puppets helped them know their voice in order to transcend their disability. As reported by the coresearchers, the children who felt silenced or unable to express themselves became aware of their voice after their association with the puppets.

The property of errors are accepted, defined as mistakes are welcomed for learning, can be directly related to Jean Piaget's (1952) research on the spiral of knowledge. One of the holistic constructivist principles as explained by Poplin (1988b) specifies that errors are an accepted part of life experiences. Learning is not effective or transformative without errors. Within the holistic constructivist teaching model, errors are acceptable as a learning tool; in fact, errors are seen as critical to learning. Data from the coresearchers confirmed this principle.

The property, an internal sense of knowing, related to the category of essence of character, is supported in the research by Piaget (1952), Poplin (1988b), and Freire (1970), who believed that children are honored for their integrity, which is the foundation for establishing their character and recognizes their individual knowledge. Children become teachers as well as learners, and are acknowledged for what they know and share. In addition to the holistic constructivist research as described previously, Brown (2004) discussed how the use of puppets in classroom instruction is a functional part of character education. Brown used shadow puppets to help children understand the concepts of character education in literature stories.

The second category of human connections—which includes *communication* and *real and make-believe* as properties—specified, according to the coresearchers, how important conversations were between the children and the puppets, the teachers and the children, and the puppeteers and the children. These conversations led to a mutual understanding so that the children would feel open to talk and experience less stigma of having a disability. The coresearchers discussed how important the puppetry performance was as it generated enthusiasm from the children that was not apparent before the children's exposure to the puppet show.

88

The literature does not directly support the aspects of the human connections category. However, research on liberatory education from Freire (1970), Freire and Macedo (1987), and Kuhn (1970) discussed the importance of changing the paradigm of how children communicate with adults and each other. Kuhn stressed the need for this new paradigm to acknowledge children as active learners, where both teachers and students can learn from each other. Although Freire's work emphasizes literacy, he stresses not only the process of learning to read but also the process of understanding the world in which one lives. The coresearchers emphasized the importance of mutual understanding for the property of communication as it is related to the category of human connection. Although the literature by Leyser (1984) and Synovitz (1999) acknowledges the use of puppets for instructional and academic practices, there does not appear to be literature that relates to the understanding of how fantasy or make-believe as represented by the puppets results in the development of effective communication. It is evident from the coresearchers' perspective that helping the children understand the concepts of real and make-believe does help them make the connection to real life. This concept needs more acknowledgment and investigation.

The third category of interactive responses includes the property *simplicity of understanding concepts*, which is related to enthusiasm and motivation for learning, as well as the property *sustained engagement*, which relates to the focus of attention. The coresearchers emphasized that the use of puppets helped the children with learning disabilities become more enthusiastic toward learning content in curriculum. They were able to sustain their attention and focus on the activities at hand. According to one coresearcher, because their ability to interact was related to the puppets, the children were actively engaged and their attention was better.

Research by Cagno and Shively (1973) supports the current study on using puppets as a motivation for learning. Cagno and Shively measured the children's responses in enthusiasm while they watched a puppet show on television. The puppetry segment was very stimulating and the preschoolers were very enthusiastic. In addition, Peck and Virkler (2006) acknowledged using puppetry in academics related to reading and literacy. They indicated that second-graders were more fluent in reading and comprehension after creating scripts for the puppet show. The scripting also helped them improve their expression when reading aloud. Additionally, Zuljevic (2005) found that puppetry used as an instructional strategy supported the social-studies content in their grade level more effectively.

The coresearchers were very specific in discussing how the use of puppetry as an instructional strategy helped the students focus their attention for a sustained period of time. The coresearchers discussed how the students were engaged in the puppet presentations and sustained that engagement for the entire show. They compared the use of puppets with a basic curriculum lesson, where students did not exhibit sustained attention. One specific coresearcher stated that the students were even fixated on the interactions with the puppets. There was a discussion from the coresearchers on how this sustained attention resulted in minimizing behavior problems.

Palumbo's (1986) research supports the coresearchers' comments on a change in children's behavior that was directly attributed to the engagement in the puppet presentation. However, the literature does not address how puppetry is used to focus the children's attention so that they are engaged in an activity for a long period of time, resulting in improved interaction with peers and adults as well as an improvement in academics. More research needs to be conducted that investigates how children with learning disabilities have a more focused and sustained attention and are internally engaged in classroom instruction after viewing a puppet show.

The fourth category of promoting creativity included the properties *increasing the dimensions of learning* and *problem solving*. This category directly related to acknowledging the students' imagination and using it to result in the action of learning. The coresearchers emphasized how they helped the children use their creativity after the children attended a puppet show. The coresearchers encouraged children and gave them opportunities to make their own puppets, and act out or mimic the puppets they watched. This activity further helped children create puppets with all kinds of disabilities. Related to the research data, the property of increasing the dimensions of learning is supported by Rugg (1963) and Wallas (1926), who suggested that the passion of the creative process is driven by emotional and spiritual connectedness. The coresearchers also emphasized that creativity is the ability to think out of the box as problem solvers. According to Rugg, the creative process starts with a problem. Leyser and Wood (1980) further substantiated this research and stressed how effective puppets were when used to problem solve. Leyser and Wood explained in their research that the purpose of a puppet show is to introduce classroom problems and provide a platform of solutions to solve these problems. One of the coresearchers discussed the process of problem solving as thinking out of the box. This results in finding another way around the problem, which folds into aspects of creativity.

The fifth category, sense of freedom, includes the properties *ongoing dialogue* and *promoting self-awareness*. The coresearchers in this study defined freedom as an acknowledgment of self that represents openness to overcoming barriers to learning. One coresearcher acknowledged the transformation of a student who verbally opened up after the puppet show by acknowledging his own disability, mirroring what one of the puppets did. Before that connection, the child was reluctant to share his true self. After the puppet expressed his willingness to share his disability, the resulting effect was the freedom of the observing child. This realization is addressed in the literature of Freire and Macedo (1987) who acknowledges the struggle that results in change. This child's experience is representative of liberating human beings from a traditional set of beliefs to an understanding that with an acceptance of self comes liberation.

The coresearchers stressed the importance of ongoing dialogue that is first established between the students and the puppets. Once the students feel comfortable interacting with puppets, they then begin, according to the coresearchers, to transfer that comfort into the classroom. This results in understanding academics and being able to socialize with their peers. One coresearcher even stressed the ability of the students to write dialogue, transferring their learning after viewing the puppet show to an academic task. This is supported by Freire (1970), who explained the practice of dialectic communication as a reflection on one's life experiences, and moving that reflection into action. Freire discussed this process of reflection and action, and referred to it as *praxis*. This can be directly related to the coresearchers' situation where the child acknowledged his own disability after reflecting on the puppet's acknowledgment of its disability. The action from the student was an acknowledgment of being comfortable to share the fact that he had the same disability.

The coresearchers demonstrated the property of promoting self-awareness as a means of promoting freedom. The coresearchers stressed that the puppets assisted the students in fostering respect, diversity, and teaching respect for disabilities. According to the coresearchers, when children are able to share information about their disabilities, there is a change in the people that surround them. This change results in other students wanting to befriend the child with the disability and inviting the child with the disability to participate in peer activities. The self-awareness that the student with the disability is supported in the literature by Sister Marilyn (1964), who found that with the use of puppets in the first grade, the children's self-confidence was enhanced while they were learning to speak English. Their nondisabled peers were then aware of the importance of being polite and reaching out for inclusion. Sister Marilyn's research specified how these children developed a greater sense of self-confidence as they succeeded in improving their English. The area of self-awareness is also related to one of the principles of holistic constructivism as described by Poplin (1988b). One of the principles of holism is the practice of self-regulating behavior. Cummins (1989) spoke extensively about self-regulating behavior for children who are bilingual when he explained the concepts of using affective filter. When students recognize their comfort level to share facts about their disability, they experience freedom; therefore, recognizing self-awareness results in a state of freedom.

Summary of Discussion

The data presented five significant categories: essence of character, human connections, interactive responses, promoting creativity, and sense of freedom. The current study acknowledges these five categories as a foundation for using puppetry as an instructional strategy for children labeled as learning disabled. The research question, "How and to what extent does the use of puppetry as a holistic constructivist pedagogy for an instructional strategy promote engagement and participation in children labeled as learning disabled?", was supported by the data. The additional question, "How and to what extent does the use of puppetry as holistic constructivist pedagogy for an instructional strategy promote social and emotional growth in children labeled as learning disabled?", was also supported by the data.

Based on the coresearchers' information and the creation of the categories and properties, there is reason to support the use of puppetry, puppet shows, and any form of puppet representations as an instructional strategy in classrooms that teach children with learning disabilities. There were two areas in the current study that were not recognized in the literature. The property of real and make-believe under the category of human connections presented a new paradigm for introducing puppetry as an instructional strategy. Another area that was limited in the literature was the property of sustained engagement, or the focus of attention, under the category of interactive responses. The current study supports the need to recognize these two areas as important for introducing and justifying puppetry as an instructional strategy for children with learning disabilities.

Implications

The introduction of puppetry as an instructional strategy is supported by the current study. The coresearchers substantiated the importance of using puppetry to open up children with learning disabilities in ways that enhance communication skills and their relationship to others, specifically peer relations. The need for ongoing dialogue that results in strong human connections is developed through the interrelationships with the use of puppets. Puppets also assist the children in their development of character with the introduction of the concept loyalty as they learn to develop friendships and be accepted by others.

The introduction of puppetry as an instructional strategy as reported in this study resulted in the children's strong self-awareness and acknowledgment of their disabilities. They learned that it is acceptable to have a disability and be able to use the process of reflection, accepting themselves and contributing to the classroom environment. Puppetry as an instructional strategy might be seen as a new paradigm for promoting engagement, participation, and social and emotional growth. Because the puppet shows are interactive and there is a tendency for the children to experience the ease of sharing, the use of puppets in the classroom would help them become more verbal about their disability. Consequently, their nondisabled peers would be more accepting of a child with a disability.

One of the most revealing results of the data included the category sense of freedom. As a concept in the classroom where children with learning disabilities might not have a sense of being free, the introduction of puppetry as an instructional strategy would enable them to have that sense of freedom. This was strongly supported by the coresearchers. When children believe their voice is heard, acknowledged, and accepted, they can begin to feel free to express themselves. Based on the coresearchers' responses, this was prevalent in the study; therefore, puppetry as an instructional strategy for children with learning disabilities is a viable tool to be incorporated in instructional practice.

Recommendations

It is recommended that puppets be created with disabilities so that they may be introduced in classrooms where students with learning disabilities are included. It is also recommended that schools find ways and opportunities to invite puppeteers with their presentations to perform. Another recommendation to assist children with learning disabilities in their acknowledgment of their disabilities is to invite the students to design and create their own puppets. This will result in a continuation of the ongoing dialogue that the current study indicates is so important. This will also give them the voice that Freire (1970), Poplin (1988b), and Piaget (1952) believed they need in order to experience liberatory education as explained by Shor and Freire (1987), and Giroux (1988b). It is recommended based on the current study that districts provide teachers with the opportunity for in-service training, supporting the use of puppets as an instructional strategy in their classrooms. Additional recommendations include more training sites for puppeteers, and possibly training retired teachers to learn the art of puppetry to mentor current teachers.

REFERENCES

Aiello, B. (1977). *Kids on the Block*. Washington, DC: Kids on the Block.

Becker, H. (1968). Behavioral science, social observation, and case studies. In D. L. Sills (Ed.), *International encyclopedia of social sciences, Vol. II* (pp. 40–41). New York: Macmillan & Free Press.

Bernier, M. (2005). Psychopuppetry: Animated symbols in therapy. In M. Bernier & J. O'Hare (Eds.), *Puppetry in education and therapy: Unlocking doors to the mind and heart* (pp. 125–133). Bloomington, IN: Authorhouse.

Berry, R. (2006). Teacher beliefs and writing instruction in two primary inclusion classrooms. *Journal of Learning Disabilities, 39*(1), 11–24.

Bogdan, R., & Biklen, S. (2007). *Qualitative research in education: An introduction of theories and methods*. Boston: Pearson Education.

Briseno, K. (2001). *From federal legislation to state regulations: A historical analysis of Illinois response to special education law*. Unpublished doctoral dissertation, Northern Illinois University, DeKalb.

Brown, S. (2004). Building character through shadow puppetry. *Art Education, 57*(6), 47–52.

Brown, W., & Meeks, J. (1997). Experimenting with the entertainment education strategy in film and video. *Journal of Film and Video, 49*(4), 30–43.

Bryant, D. (2003, Spring). Introduction to special issue: Promoting effective instruction for struggling secondary students. *Learning Disability Quarterly, 26*(1), 70–71.

Cagno, D., & Shively, J. (1973). *Children's reactions to segments of a children's television series*. Charleston, WV: Appalachia Educational Laboratory.

Chen, F. (2003). Shadow theaters of the world. *Asian Folklore Studies, 62*(1), 25–64.

Creswell, J. (2003). *Qualitative, quantitative, and mixed methods approaches*. Thousand Oaks, CA: Sage.

Cummins, J. (1989). *Empowering minority students*. Sacramento: California Association for Bilingual Education.

Davis, L., Larkin, E., & Graves, S. (2002). Intergenerational learning through play. *International Journal of Early Childhood, 34*(2), 42–49.

Dinkmeyer, D. (1970). *Developing understanding of self and others*. Circle Pines, MN: American Guidance Service.

Dunn, L., Horton, K., & Smith, J. (1968). *Peabody language development kits*. Circle Pines, MN: American Guidance Service.

Forness, S. (1988). Reductionism paradigm shifts and learning disabilities. *Journal of Learning Disabilities, 21*(7), 421–424.

Fowles, B., & Voyat, G. (1974). Piaget meets Big Bird: Is television a passive teacher? *The Urban Review, 7*(1), 69–80.

Freire, P. (1970). *Pedagogy of the oppressed*. New York: Continuum Press.

Freire, P. (1973). *Education for critical consciousness*. New York: Seabury Press.

Freire, P., & Macedo, D. (1987). *Reading the word and the world*. South Hadley, MA: Bergin & Garvey.

Gardner, H. (1993). *Multiple intelligences: Theory in practice*. New York: Basic Books.

Getzels, J., & Csikszentmihalyi, M. (1976). *The creative vision*. New York: John Wiley & Sons.

Giroux, H. (1988a). *Schooling and the struggle for public life: Critical pedagogy in the modern age*. Minneapolis: University of Minnesota Press.

Giroux, H. (1988b). *Teachers as intellectuals: Toward a critical pedagogy of learning*. Westport, CN: Bergine Garvey.

Gorn, S. (1977). *What do I do when: The answer book on individual education programs*. Horsham, PA: LRP.

Gronna, S., Serna, L., Kennedy, C., & Prater, M. (1999). Promoting generalized social interactions using puppets and script: Training in an integrated preschool. *Behavior Modification, 23*(3), 419–440.

Hallahan, D., & Cruickshank, W. (1973). *Psychoeducational foundations of learning disabilities*. Englewood Cliff, NJ: Prentice Hall.

Hammill, D., & Bartel, N. (1971). *Educational perspectives in learning disabilities*. New York: John Wiley & Sons.

Hancock, D., & Algozzine, B. (2006). *Doing case study research: A practical guide for beginning research*. New York: Teachers College Press.

Haring, N., & Bateman, B. (1977). *Teaching the learning disabled child*. Englewood Cliffs, NJ: Prentice Hall.

Hayward, D., Das, J., & Janzen, T. (2007). Innovative programs for improvement in reading through cognitive enhancement: A remediation study. *Canadian First Nations Children, 40*(5), 443–475.

Hearne, D., & Stone, S. (1995). Multiple intelligences and underachievement: Lessons from individuals with learning disabilities. *Journal of Learning Disabilities, 28*(7), 439–448.

Hearne, J., Poplin, M., Schoneman, C., & O'Shauchnessy, E. (1988). Computer aptitude: An investigation of differences among junior high students with learning disabilities and their non-learning disabled peers. *Journal of Learning Disabilities, 21*(8), 489–492.

Henley, M., Ramsey, R., & Algozzine, R. (2002). *Characteristics of and strategies for teaching students with mild disabilities*. Boston, MA: Allyn & Bacon

Heshusius, L. (1986). The Newtonian mechanistic paradigm special education and contours of alternatives: An overview. *Journal of Learning Disabilities, 22*(7), 403–415.

Hirshelwood, J. (1917). *Congenital word blindness*. London: Lewis.

Jackson, J. (1915). On the physiology of language. *Brain, 38*(1), 39–64.

Jordan, A., & Stavovich, P. (2003). Teachers' personal epistemological beliefs about students with disabilities as indicators of effective teaching practices. *Journal of Research in Special Education Needs, 3*(1), 1–14.

Jung, C. (1970). *Archetypes and the collective unconscious*. Buenos Aires, Argentina: Paidos.

Katz, L., Stone, C., Carlisle, J., Corey, D., & Zeng, J. (2008). Initial progress of children identified with disabilities in Michigan's reading first schools. *Exceptional Children, 74*(2), 235–256.

Keel, M., Dangel, H., & Owens, S. (1999). Selecting instructional interventions for students with mild disabilities in inclusive classrooms. *Focus on Exceptional Children, 31*(8), 1–16.

Keough, B. (2005, Spring). Revisiting classification and identification. *Learning Disability Quarterly, 28*(2), 100–102.

Kimball, W., & Heron, T. (1988). A behavioral commentary on Poplin's discussion of reductionistic fallacy and holistic constructivist principles. *Journal of Learning Disabilities, 21*(7), 425–447.

Kline, S., & Stewart, K., Murphy, D. (2006). Media literacy in the risk society: Toward a risk reduction strategy. *Canadian Journal of Education, 29*(1), 131–153.

Kruger, M. (2004, September). *Puppets in entertainment education: Universal principles and African performance traditions as a model for interaction.* Presentation at Fourth International Entertainment Education Conference, Capetown, South Africa.

Kuhn, T. (1970). *The structure of scientific revolution.* University of Chicago Press.

Lerner, J. (1971). *Children with learning disabilities.* Boston: Houghton Mifflin.

Lesser, G. (1974). *Children and television: Lessons from* Sesame Street. New York: Vintage Books/Random House.

Lewis, R., & Doorlag, D. (2006). *Teaching special education children in the mainstream* (7th ed.). Boston: Allyn & Bacon.

Leyser, Y. (1984). Educational puppetry: A valuable instructional resource in regular and special education. *The Pointer, 28*(3), 33–36.

Leyser, Y., & Wood, J. (1980). An evaluation of puppet interaction in a second grade classroom. *Education, 100*(3), 292–296.

Lovett, B., & Lewandowski, L. (2006). Gifted students with learning disabilities: Who are they? *Journal of Learning Disabilities, 39*(6), 515–527.

Lowe, J., & Matthew, K. (2000). Puppets and prose. *Science and Children, 37*(8), 41–43.

Mann, L. (1979). *On the trail of process: A historical perspective on cognitive processes and their training.* New York: Grune & Stratton.

Mazzarella Bros. (Producers.) (2001). *The American puppet: A history of puppetry in America* [Video recording]. Bristol, CT: Producers.

McLaren, P. (1989). *Life in schools: An introduction to critical pedagogy in the foundations of education.* White Plains, NY: Longman.

Mercer, C., & Mercer, A. (2005). *Teaching students with learner problems* (7th ed.). Upper Saddle River, NJ: Pearson/Merrill Prentice Hall.

Merriam, S. (2001). *Qualitative research and case study: Applications in education*. San Francisco: Jossey-Bass.

Mueller, T., Singer, G., & Grace, E. (2004). Individuals With Disabilities Education Act and California's Prop. 227: Implications for English language learners with special needs. *Bilingual Research Journal, 28*(2), 231–251.

Myers, P., & Hammill, D. (1976). *Methods for learning disorders*. New York: John Wiley & Sons.

Myklebust, H. (ED) (1968). *Progress in learning disabilities*. New York: Grune & Stratton.

National Dissemination Center for Children With Disabilities. (2004). *Building the legacy. The National Information Center for Children and Youth With Disabilities*. Washington, DC: Author.

Palumbo, A. (1986). *Puppetry with profoundly handicapped children*. Providence, RI: Puppetry Workshop.

Peck, S., & Virkler, A. (2006). Reading in the shadows: Extending literacy skills through shadow-puppet theatre. *The Reading Teacher, 59*(8), 786–795.

Piaget, J. (1952). *The origins of intelligence in children*. New York: W.W. Norton Co.

Piaget, J. (1954). *The construction of reality in the child*. New York: Basic Books.

Pierangelo, R. (2003). *The special educator's book of lists*. San Francisco: Jossey-Bass.

Poplin, M. (1988a). Holistic/constructivist principles of the teaching and learning process: Implications for the field of learning disabilities. *The Journal of Learning Disabilities, 21*(7), 401–416.

Poplin, M. (1988b). The reductionistic fallacy in learning disabilities; replicating the past by reducing the present. *The Journal of Learning Disabilities, 21*(7), 389–400.

Poplin, M., & Cousin, P. (1996). *Alternative views of learning disabilities: Issues for the 21st century*. Austin, TX: PRO-ED.

Poplin, M., & Stone, S. (1992). Paradigm shifts in instructional strategies: From reductionism to holistic constructivism. In W. Stainback & S. Stainback (Eds.), *Controversial issues confronting special education* (pp. 153–179). Boston: Allyn & Bacon.

Porshan, F. (1980). *The puppet traditions of Sub-Saharan Africa: Descriptions and definitions.* Austin: University of Texas Press.

Pub. L. No. 94-142, 20 U.S.C. 1415 § 615 (e) (3) (1975).

Rugg, H. (1963). *Imagination.* New York: Harper & Row.

Ryndak, D., & Alper, S. (2003). *Curriculum and instruction for students with significant disabilities in inclusive settings.* Boston: Pearson Educational.

Schuster, J. (1985). Ten years later: PL 94-142 and the building principle. *Education, 106*(2), 231–238. Retrieved from Academic Search Premier database.

Shor, I., & Freire, P. (1987). *A pedagogy for liberation.* Granby, MA: Bergin & Garvey.

Simmons, D., Kameenui, E., & Chard, D. (1998). General education teachers' assumptions about learning and students with learning disabilities: Design of instructional analysis. *Learning Disability Quarterly, 21*(1), 6–21.

Sister Marilyn. (1964). Puppets build self-confidence. *Catholic School Journal, 64*(5), 55–56.

Skrit, T., Harris, K., & Shriner, J. (2000). *Special education policy and practice: Accountability, instruction, and social changes.* Denver, CO: Love.

Smith, L. (2005). Social competency skills through puppetry. In M. Bernier & J. O'Hare (Eds.), *Puppetry in education and therapy: Unlocking doors to the mind and heart* (pp. 83–86). Bloomington, IN: Authorhouse.

Sorrells, A., Rieth, H., & Sindelar, P. (2004). *Critical issues in special education: Access to diversity and accountability.* Boston: Pearson Education.

Stake, R. (1995). *The art of case study research.* Thousand Oaks, CA: Sage.

Stevens, S. (1980). *The learning disabled child: Ways that parents can help.* Winston-Salem, NC: John F. Blair.

Stone, S. (1992). *Divergent thinking: Nontraditional or creative talents of monolingual, bilingual, and special education students in an elementary school.* Unpublished doctoral dissertation, Claremont Graduate School of Education, CA.

Synovitz, L. (1999). Using puppetry in a coordinated school health program. *The Journal of School Health, 69*(4), 145–147.

U.S. Department of Education. (2006). *IDEA '97 amendments, final regulations.* Retrieved on July 14, 2009, from http://www.ed.gov/policy/speced/reg/ regulations.html

U.S. Office of Education. (1977). *Assistance to states for education for handicapped children procedures for evaluating specific learning disabilities. Federal Registry*, 42, G1082–G1085.

Wallas, G. (1926). *The art of thought.* New York: Harcourt Brace & Co.

Warner, M., & Sather-Bull, K. (1986). Grounding learning disabled definitions and practices in systems of educational thought. *Journal of Learning Disabilities, 19*(3), 139–143.

Whitehead, A. (1978). *Process and reality.* New York: Free Press.

Whitmore, J., & Maker, S. (1985). *The intellectual giftedness in disabled persons.* Rockville, MD: Aspen Systems.

Wiederholt, J. (1974). Historical perspectives on the education of the learning disabled. In L. Mann & S. Sabatino (Eds.), *The second review of special education* (pp. 103–153). Philadelphia: JSE Press.

Wiest, D., & Kriel, D. (1995). Transformational obstacles in special education. *Journal of Learning Disabilities, 28*(7), 399–407.

Wolfensberger, W. (2003). *Leadership and change in human service: Selected reading from Wolf Wolfensberger.* New York: Routledge.

Wong, B. (1988). An instructional model for intervention research in learning disabilities. *Learning Disabilities Research, 4*(1), 5–16.

Yin, R. (1994). *Case study research: Design methods* (2nd ed.). Thousand Oaks, CA: Sage.

Ysseldyke, J., Algozzine, B., & Thurlow, M. (2000). *Critical issues in special education* (3rd ed). Boston: Houghton Mifflin.

Zuljevic, V. (2005). Puppets—A great addition to everyday teaching. *Thinking Classroom, 6*(1), 37–44.